**Addiction, Crime, and Social
Policy**

Addiction, Crime, and Social Policy

Philip C. Baridon
PRC Public Management
Services, Inc.

Lexington Books
D.C. Heath and Company
Lexington, Massachusetts
Toronto   London

Library of Congress Cataloging in Publication Data

Baridon, Philip C
    Addiction, crime, and social policy.

    Bibliography: p. 113
    Includes index.
    1. Drug abuse and crime. I. Title.
HV5801.B34   364.2'54   75-32221
ISBN 0-669-00342-5

Copyright © 1976 by D.C. Heath and Company

Published simultaneously in Canada

Printed in the United States of America

International Standard Book Number: 0-669-00342-5

Library of Congress Catalog Card Number: 75-32221

To Andrea

Contents

List of Figure and Tables

Preface

Over 60 years have passed since the decision to criminalize non-medical opiate use. Since then the relationship between addiction and the crime that is widely associated with it has become a major social issue. This book is an exploratory attempt to analyze certain aspects of that relationship.

A principal task is to construct retrospectively the criminal career and drug usage patterns for a sample of addicts through intensive interviews. As part of this process of outlining careers, very specific inquiries are made about the nature of some of the social and economic ties between addiction and crime. Among the questions considered are (1) the economic impact of rising heroin prices on both the decision making of the addict and the level of property offenses, and (2) the nature and extent of preaddictive criminal behavior and the mechanism through which addiction intensifies this activity. These relationships are explored in depth, using crime statistics, police records, published literature, and interview data.

Findings include the discovery of a powerful inverse relationship between the retain price of heroin and the level of reported property offenses over a period of several years. It is hypothesized that a deteriorating heroin market, increased law enforcement resources, and a newly available methadone program produced the association. From the addicts' view a critical element in this association is the steadily declining purity of heroin. (Future research may be able to demonstrate that this is a critical variable for the success of treatment programs in retaining addicts and reducing crime.)

A somewhat related finding is that monetary cost is largely irrelevant in the addicts' decision whether a habit has grown unmanageable and whether treatment is personally indicated. Benefits seem directly related to the quality of the drug and, therefore, the "high," while costs are measured more in terms of sustained criminal involvement and social isolation than in terms of cash to finance the habit.

A strong relationship was discovered in which the appearance of a given type of offense *prior to* opiate addiction is an almost certain predictor of its postaddiction use as a means of support. The importance of this sequence for those interested in prevention is considerable. The appearance of serious crimes such as robbery and burglary, and the increasing use of opiates should sound clear warning of future involvement.

Finally, the criminogenic effects of criminalizing nonmedical opiate use are documented and discussed. While intensification of earlier crime patterns is the usual means of adjustment to addiction, many previously uninvolved in criminal activity experience radical changes in their life-styles. It is suggested that this situation of producing one type of deviance through attempts to control another should be remedied by a reexamination of social and legal priorities.

Acknowledgments

I want to express my deep gratitude to several people whose unselfish assistance made this work possible. Professor Hans Toch of the School of Criminal Justice, The State University of New York at Albany, consistently offered crucial advice and support. Also, the role of Sherwood McGinnis of The American University Computer Center as an intermediary between me and "The Machine" was of inestimable aid. Through all phases of this effort, from interviewing to indexing, my wife, Andrea, has been a constant source of aid and encouragement. Her tireless and uncomplaining reading, editing, and typing of so many drafts was a blessing.

Introduction

Serious efforts to control opiate addiction began after the turn of the century. Over the years, a variety of arguments have been advanced to justify the need for this control: Addiction is an immoral and degrading vice; it produces a population that is dangerous both to itself and to others; it creates significant economic losses through morbidity and accidents; and it promotes increased crime among opiate abusers. While any of these may constitute sufficient grounds for disapproval, it is the last item—the link between addiction and crime—that is the most visible and the most emotional.

This book is an exploratory effort to analyze certain aspects of that link. Not only the nature and extent of the relationship, but also the mechanisms that seem to bind it together come under scrutiny. This research attempts to promote more understanding of such questions as how, why, and for whom crime has become a consequence of addiction. The focus here is to identify and relate the more important legal, cultural, and economic forces that appear to dictate the parameters of the relationship between opiate addiction and crime. In essence, the result of these various forces *is* our social policy toward addiction, and we will characterize and examine some of its effects, discovered through in-depth interviews of 101 heroin addicts and through other available data sources.

An exhaustive analysis of all possible aspects of this relationship would be quite beyond the scope of a single effort. Therefore, a more limited number of relevant concerns have been developed that are considered both researchable and important. Although some tangential material also is presented, the focus of the inquiry centers around the issues outlined below.[a]

Principal Issues

1. Is there a stable and positive correlation between the price of opiates and gainful crime within the same geographical area?

If, indeed, many property crimes are committed only to obtain money for narcotics, one would expect a sharp increase in drug prices to precipitate some sort of increase in the gainful crimes of

---

[a] For purposes of this study, *addiction* is defined as the daily use of heroin or any other opiate.

addicts. In other words, would such a rise in prices in an area with a large addict population not cause a corresponding increase in property offenses?

2. What is the addicts' personal response to spiraling drug costs?

Is it reasonable to postulate a relatively fixed but unknown price range of daily costs above which even the most confirmed addict-criminals must engage in *additional* gainful crime, but below which drug costs are merely deducted from the profits of an ongoing pattern of illicit and gainful activity? The recent rise in daily costs in Washington, D.C. from $25 to $56 per day does not appear to have caused any such increase in gainful crime; nor did any cost-related crime fluctuations occur in New York, where addicts entering methadone maintenance had mean daily drug costs of $74. This undertaking lists and evaluates the range of reported responses to increasing drug costs not only for the sample, but also for other addicts as perceived by the sample respondents.

3. Is there any evidence that our drug control policies may be creating additional deviance?

Given the frequently reported intensification of crime following addiction, a significant question becomes, to what extent does present social policy on narcotics control force the marginal or youthful deviate to "graduate" to a pattern of extensive criminal activity? In other words, as a result of opiate addiction, what *additional* proportion make that transition who otherwise would have remained marginal or even drifted out?

4. What is the role of age in the interdependence of addiction and crime?

It is hypothesized that the earlier the onset of addiction, the more extensive will be the young addict's contact with the criminal subculture, and the less likely will be his socialization into a conventional life-style. In other words, age at addiction onset and criminal activity during addiction should vary inversely.

5. What is the nature and extent of preaddictive crime?

While the available literature indicates that at least some deviance is usually a prerequisite to narcotics use, little is known about the relative distribution of this activity by type and frequency.

6. What differences exist between addict and nonaddict crime?

It seems reasonable that the fact of addiction would impose certain constraints upon the type of crime selected, the frequency of commission, or the opportunity structure within which the addict operates. What, for example, is the addict's perception of the qualitative and quantitative differences between the crime committed by him and by his nonaddict peers? Does the daily requirement of money to support the habit give the addict less time to plan his crimes? Does the addict believe that the effects of the drug render him less capable of either planning or executing his offenses? Is the addict forced to take additional risks that nonaddict criminals would avoid because of the time constraints imposed by his habit?

What are the implications to be found by systematically exploring these related questions? If, for example, this study reveals that relatively more members of an addict group than a similar nonaddict group "graduate" to a pattern of extensive crime, then the explanation would appear to lie in our social control policies. On the other hand, if the interview and arrest data show that most addicts are involved in substantial, gainful crime prior to addiction, then no such inferences about drug control policy and crime would be appropriate.

The interview items on drug costs and how addicts handle that problem should provide some insights into the addicts' decision making and how that process is affected by law enforcement. A finding that addicts are more likely to intensify crime as a response to rising drug costs would have very different implications than a finding that most seek treatment in an effort to control their habit, and, therefore, their expenses. Also, differences in the types of crime committed by addicts and nonaddicts should in part be dependent upon social policy decisions, which dictate how one lives as an addict. If, for example, one were both a thief and an addict in a culture in which heroin were legally available, then the patterns of addict crime should resemble those of nonaddict crime.

Finally, any discussion of the life-style of addiction touches all of these concerns. It is shaped by social policy, drug costs, recruitment patterns, etc.

Methodology

Two primary data sources are used in developing and discussing the relationships under study.

First, to provide the necessary control to demonstrate the nature and magnitude of any criminogenic effect that our drug control policies may have on addicts' criminal careers, it was necessary to draw a systematic random sample of 60 records from the arrest files in a large urban police department on the East Coast of the United States. Each contained a chronological list of all police charges. Only adults between the ages of 18 and 35 were sampled to insure a valid comparison to the addict population. Ten of these 60 were excluded because of drug charges. The remaining were divided into two categories based upon the *seriousness* of offenses and their *patterns over time*. Forty-one individuals were found to be "marginal criminals" and nine to be "confirmed criminals." (This simple dichotomous classificatory scheme will be useful somewhat later.)

Second, a nonrandom sample of 101 addicts currently registered with the Narcotics Treatment Administration (NTA) in Washington, D.C. has been interviewed in depth. NTA was selected for two reasons: (1) It is by far the largest such agency in the area. All other facilities combined have a capacity of fewer than 200 addicts compared with the 2,400 now on NTA rolls; and (2) with its large size and diverse population, NTA is most likely to represent the identifiable types of addicts in the metropolitan area. The usual sources—the prison, the probation agency, and the voluntary treatment agency—tend to have a somewhat different type of addict. NTA, on the other hand, accepts probationers, paroled offenders, and walk-in volunteers.

Developing a usable, structured questionnaire was necessary for this undertaking. No standardized instrument is available that focuses so narrowly on the relationship between addiction and crime; and no series of unstructured interviews would have allowed any quantitative precision. The original instrument was found to be quite inadequate. Questions frequently required rephrasing, and the previously developed set of responses often were either inappropriate or incomplete. In some cases the addicts themselves suggested new questions or the rephrasing of old ones. Six people were interviewed using the original draft and eight on the second draft. This latter edition was much more satisfactory and required only modest changes to insure a relatively unambiguous communication.

One of the most serious problems in making revisions was to keep effective questions short and simple. The ability of the addicts to remember and to concentrate was almost uniformly poor. Most did not finish high school and few had sufficiently developed verbal skills to allow more complex questioning. In some cases, what appeared to be a basic deficiency in this area was compounded by the influence of medication. In addition to methadone, addicts were occasionally given sedative-hypnotic drugs, which also impair concentration. Following pretesting, a total of 101 respondents were interviewed.

The possibility of taping these conversations was seriously considered. After the adoption of the present instrument, I taped a few interviews and attempted to tape others. Given the sensitive nature of the questions being asked, the presence of a tape recorder seemed offensive to most of the addicts. They were extremely suspicious, and it quickly became obvious that its use would reduce both the candor of the interviews and the number of them.

A very obvious and critical concern is the veracity of the addicts, particularly on such a sensitive matter as criminal activity. Only two practical means of checking responses suggest themselves. One of these is the impression of the interviewer, particularly when discrepancies are brought (as tactfully as possible) to the attention of the respondent. (Two interviews were discarded from the sample because of obviously false responses.) The other method used consists of a 15 percent systematic random sample of the criminal records of the participants.

Beginning with a random selection between one and seven (five in this case), the official criminal record of every seventh respondent was made available through the NTA identification numbers. Fourteen such records were supplied and appear in appendix C, where they are compared with the self-report data on arrests. The substantive agreement is generally close. A few recent (1973-74) charges that were acknowledged by the respondents do not appear on the record because of either time lag or the known fact that records are often "pulled" pending the disposition of a charge. A few additional reported charges that do not appear are explained by the fact that these are D.C. records only. Arrest and prosecution information from other jurisdictions would not be listed. Records from neighboring jurisdictions are not available. Agreement about the year of arrest tends to deteriorate as the time frame recedes, but is usually close. In some cases, the technical charges are comparable but not identical. Narcotics vagrancy, for example, is sometimes confused with possession of narcotics.

In sum, agreement could be considered poor in only one case and marginal in one more of the 14 comparisons. Significantly, in no case was there any extensive criminal record not acknowledged by the respondent. Attempted burglary (a misdemeanor) was the *most* serious charge that any respondent failed to acknowledge. The most common form of disparity occurred when the official listing was less complete than the self-report listing.

**Addiction, Crime, and Social
Policy**

1

An Overview of Opiate Addiction and Crime

This chapter explores through the literature a number of background issues that are considered important. It is a synthesis of historical, legal, medical, economic, and cross-cultural perspectives on the relationship of addiction and crime. In addition to data on the current situation in this country, some cross-cultural and historical analysis was attempted from the available literature. The criminal role of opiate addicts as they appear in other places and other times has considerable value in placing in perspective the criminal addicts' present status in the United States. Also included below is a logical typology of addict roles to facilitate the later analysis and discussion of data.

Social Policy and the Belief That Addiction Causes Crime

As early as 1900 (14 years before the Harrison Narcotic Act), the influential American Medical Association (AMA) began suggesting that addicts were constantly involved in "crimes of selfishness, impulse, and cunning,"[1] In 1916 the AMA stated bluntly in an article entitled "The Drug Habit and the Underworld" that "ninety-five per cent (of the addicts) are criminals *by reason of* the acquired habit."[2] Seven years later, the same journal restated its position by concluding that "contrary to popular belief, the vast majority of narcotic habitués are criminals." There were few official voices raised in opposition to such suggestions. Indeed, the opium addict did seem a different and sinister sort of character. It was precisely during this time (1919-22) that a series of three Supreme Court cases made the self-fulfilling prophecy linking addiction and crime possible.[3] The Court interpretations of the Harrison Narcotic Act had effectively eliminated for the time any participation of the medical profession in the treatment or rehabilitation of addicts. The few doctors who had been willing to prescribe narcotics to addicts

1

became thoroughly cowed by the successful criminal prosecution of their peers.

Law enforcement, meanwhile, continued to intensify. By 1925 the Treasury Department, with the vocal support of a conservative AMA, had shut down the last of 44 clinics for registered addicts.[4] The addict was finally an outlaw. Indiana even passed a law prohibiting the appearance of an addict in any public place.[5] Other states not only outlawed possession and use but made it a criminal offense to *be* an addict. It was not until 1962[6] that this latter offense category was struck down by the Supreme Court.

The change in social policy began to be felt during the latter half of the 1920s. Minority involvement was increasing. Middle-class, middle-aged white females were being replaced by lower class black males as the modal category of addicts. The mean age of both experimentation and addiction also began to fall; it was no longer a vice of the middle-aged.[7] Racial fears seemed to aggravate a growing belief that addicts were increasingly involved in crime. In a national radio broadcast on March 1, 1928, NBC compared addiction with leprosy and stated that:

Most of the daylight robberies, daring holdups, cruel murders, and similar crimes of violence are now known to be committed chiefly by drug addicts, who constitute the primary cause of our alarming crime wave.[8]

In 1932 the Chicago District Attorney's Office emphasized its opinion that addicts were criminals and that the Harrison Act was finally stemming the flow of narcotics.[9] During this general period, there appeared to be consensus on the fact that the addict was a criminal but little agreement as to why. One writer suggested that "the drug itself" produced the deviance and that "the dope fiend is involved in the commission of major crimes, including theft, rape, kidnapping, and murder. . . ."[10]

While recent writings have become somewhat more sophisticated, the belief that addiction causes crime remains unshaken. To the satisfaction of most present observers, the connection between addiction and property crimes seems well enough established. A 1972 national survey by the National Commission on Marihuana and Drug Abuse (Shafer Commission) revealed that 90 percent of the American people believe that heroin addicts commit substantial crime they would not otherwise commit. All that seems to remain is a rather interesting numbers game. Some researchers have suggested that the addict must steal property amounting to between two and one-half to five times the actual cost of his habit,[11] and that on a yearly basis, this would amount to between \$25,000 and \$50,000.[12]

Aggregate estimates of the cost of addict crime are even more interesting.

Since half of all property and monetary thefts occur in large cities where junkies are concentrated, and one-half of all these crimes are committed by addicts, a figure of \$250 million (annually) for total addict thefts in the United States is not unreasonable.[13]

The above figure appears to be based on the belief that there are about 200,000 addicts in the United States. As of December 31, 1972 the Bureau of Narcotics and Dangerous Drugs (BNDD) informs us that there are over 626,000 active addicts, a *rate* about 15 percent higher than when heroin was sold over the counter in drug stores!

The political implications of such costs have scarcely gone unnoticed. In 1956, after seven months of study involving more than 345 witnesses, a Senate judiciary subcommittee investigating narcotics addiction and illicit drug traffic in the United States concluded that "approximately 50% of all crime in U.S. cities and 25% of all crime in the nation was attributable to drug addiction." In his 1972 campaign, Senator Edmund Muskie reiterated the above findings and further stated that the narcotic habit costs us "billions of dollars in stolen money each year."[14]

The mandate to law enforcement is clear: eliminate illicit narcotic use and a large part of the "crime problem" will solve itself. Typical of such beliefs is an article in *Police* magazine, which concluded that "overall crime should decrease 40-60% if street drugs were not available."[15] In 1972 a San Francisco methadone conference stated that the "huge volume of drug-related crime in New York City has created a mass fear of addicts" and that one-half the new admissions to the city's jails are arrested addicts.[16]

Medical, Historical, and Cross-cultural Indications That Opiate Addiction and Crime Are Not Necessarily Related

If addiction and crime are causally related, it must be either through a direct criminogenic effect of the opiate itself or through some more indirect social mechanism. This former possibility, believed to be much less important, is dealt with in the following section.

The Psychopharmacology of the Opiates

There are approximately 98 opiate drugs listed among the three schedules of the 1961 United Nations Single Convention on Narcotic Drugs.[17] The pharmacological effect of any of these drugs is essentially similar, the major difference being in potency, duration of effect, and rapidity of tolerance. It is not improper, therefore, for the purposes of this study to combine opiates into a single class.

Heroin (diacetyl morphine) was not developed until 1874; yet, it is clearly the principal opiate of abuse today.[18] Considering the general acceptance of such opiates as methadone and morphine by the medical profession, the fear that seems to be generated by heroin is without any physiological basis. Heroin is, in fact, rapidly converted by the body into monacetyl morphine. All major pharmacological actions of heroin are due to the morphine that is released from it in the brain.[19] Addicts who were administered subcutaneous injections of heroin and morphine could not distinguish them.[20] Furthermore, published autopsies and other tests have failed to demonstrate any primary pathologies or long-term organic damage associated with opiate use.[21]

The administration of opiates generally results in feelings of euphoria, drowsiness, inability to concentrate, and lethargy.[22] The hyperactivity and paranoid behavior that often results from cocaine or amphetamine abuse is rare.[23]

Violent crime by addicts also is believed to be rare. The Shafer Commission states that "users of opiates are significantly *less likely* to commit homicide, rape, and assault than are users of alcohol, amphetamines, and barbiturates."[24]

The abstinence syndrome (withdrawal) following cessation of use is well known. Either the sickness or the fear of it may encourage crime as a means of obtaining money to relieve withdrawal. In some sense this constitutes a criminogenic effect directly attributable to opiate abuse. On the other hand, the fact that opiates for nonmedical use are both expensive and scarce is directly the result of social policy. Whether withdrawal as a consequence of physical dependence produces crime seems to be more a question of the legal status of opiates than of their pharmacological characteristics.

One additional area exists that might directly link instrumental crime with addiction. It could be argued that the protracted depressant effects of opiates would make work difficult and sufficient motivation unlikely. Crime then becomes a likely means of support. Two objections may be raised to this scenario. In the first place, tolerance to those depressant effects does develop sufficiently to allow many addicts to work at a broad variety of jobs. A partial list of some of the occupations reported in this study is found in chapter 3. More importantly, it is very difficult to posit any causal direction in this matter. It is eminently reasonable to suggest that those who not only experiment but allow themselves to become addicted to a narcotic lack the initial motivation to strive and to succeed in a conventional work setting. Lack of motivation then becomes a precursor to opiate abuse rather than an effect of it.

In sum, there appears to be little in the literature that would indicate any direct criminogenic effects from opiate use.

Indirect Evidence of the Relationship Between Addiction and Crime

If there is any necessary relationship between addiction and criminal activity, it should become apparent through either historical or cross-cultural analysis.

Alfred Lindesmith has traced the history of opium use by man from the time of the Sumerians through the nineteenth century in Massachusetts. He suggests that even though its use was widespread during the last century, addiction was not importantly linked with crime. Intelligent and respected citizens were often users; many thought of opium smokers as "sporting characters."[25] In an 1881 article in *Catholic World* the author concluded that narcotics addiction was an unfortunate moral sickness that could be overcome by sufficient will power. No mention is made of criminal or antisocial behavior.[26] In 1915 *American Medicine* stressed that addiction was a medical problem rather than a police problem. The only abuse they noted was that the illicit sale and distribution of narcotics increasingly involved criminal elements. This latter trend had just begun, since the Harrison Act had been law for less than a year. A

1919 article in the *New Orleans Medical Journal* sharply criticized the sudden harsh implementation of the Harrison Act. They also noted, based on data from their clinic, that "only a small portion are true criminals." Evidently the addict profile was in transition at this time, since it also was observed that the social origins of the addicts were unusually diverse.[27]

This time was a period of transition in other respects. Drug abuse was now defined more as a social rather than a personal problem. In 1919 a special committee of the Treasury Department to investigate drug traffic began a program of adverse publicity, claiming that drug addicts were a widespread social problem. With the creation of the Federal Bureau of Narcotics in 1930, two simultaneous attacks on the addict were intensified: one to cut him off from medical help, the other to define him as a moral degenerate and a criminal.[28]

Some research on crime and drugs nevertheless continued. A 1922 Boston study of "morphinism" (as it was then called) revealed that one-third of a sample of 60 addicts had been arrested for non-drug offenses prior to the onset of addiction. They also noted that nondrug arrests tended to increase following addiction.[29]

Three years later a psychiatric study of 225 addicts concluded that "in the vast majority of cases" the addict was a criminal before he became addicted. No relationship to violent crime was found. They stated that both heroin and morphine would "change drunken, fighting psychopaths into sober, non-aggressive idlers."[30]

Older foreign studies, although replete with methodological difficulties, generally indicate no relationship between addiction and crime.

In one study, a retrospective analysis of 44 Norwegian addicts showed that "addiction does not seem to play an important role in criminality."[31] The *Indian Journal of Medical Research* stated that the habit of eating opium has no direct relationship to crime and is not socially objected to in India.[32] A 1955 United Nations study of India reiterated almost the same findings but added that opium smoking was considered to be *less* injurious than alcohol abuse.[33]

Although these studies are only suggestive, they are typical of the literature of the times. The next section continues to explore the problem as it exists in a foreign but industrially developed nation. Great Britain was chosen for three reasons: (1) There is more quality research done on the problem than elsewhere in western Europe; (2) it is socially and culturally the most similar to the United States;

and (3) their policy of narcotics control is and has been quite different from ours.

This last item requires some elaboration. Federal law in the form of the Drug Abuse Control Act of 1970 strictly proscribes the use of certain drugs. Heroin in this country is a "Schedule I" drug, which means that no lawful use is permitted other than limited experimentation.[34] In contrast, heroin—the drug of choice for most addicts—is dispensed by British clinics at a cost to the addict of 24 cents a week.[35] Furthermore, in most clinics the addict is allowed the additional euphoria obtained by using a syringe—a practice forbidden in the United States. The United Kingdom also has no compulsory commitment laws for addicts. Unlike many jurisdictions within the United States, the mere status of being an addict does not permit involuntary civil incarceration.[36] In sum, the essence of the difference in approach of the two policies appears to lie in the more medical and less punitive methods of the United Kingdom.

The Relationship in an European Country Utilizing a Nonpunitive Approach to Control

In 1912 The Hague Convention laid the foundation for the international control of narcotics. The American response was the Harrison Narcotic Act two years later. Great Britain waited 14 years before committing itself to a national policy. The 1926 report of the Ministry of Health Committee on Morphine and Heroin Addiction (the Rolleston Committee) concluded that addiction "must be regarded as a manifestation of disease and not as a mere form of vicious indulgence." While the means of implementing this belief have changed greatly over the years, it still remains the principal tenet of the "British System."

At no time have the British had more than 3,000 addicts. That peak occurred early in 1970 and has shown a gradual (8 percent) decline since then.[37] This compares quite favorably with the current American estimate. When both countries are reduced to a standard rate, the problem in the United States is approximately 50 times as severe as in the United Kingdom.

In addition to limiting the spread of addiction, the approach of the British government appears to have obviated the need for the deep interdependence of the addict and criminal subcultures so characteristic of the American scene. This is not to say that British addicts do not engage in crime; it does mean that the nature and extent of criminality among British addicts is substantially different from that of their American counterparts.

A significant but indirect form of evidence for this lies in the sharp differences in addict profiles. While the confirmed criminal seems to be the modal category for American addicts, the British addicts generally seem to live conventional life-styles except for addiction. Rather than being from lower class and disadvantaged ghettoes, Dr. David Hawks of the London Addiction Research Unit describes them as "'middle-class drop-outs' whose addiction, far from being explicable in terms of some material disadvantage, appears to have been motivated by the deliberate rejection of middle-class norms and opportunities." A similar finding recently was reported in the *Bulletin on Narcotics*:

The distribution of the male patients among the various social classes was found to differ little from that of the general population, but among the females there was a slightly higher proportion than expected whose fathers were in the professional and intermediate occupations.[38]

The pattern of criminal activity among British addicts is both quantitatively and qualitatively different from that of their American counterparts. A survey by the Department of Health and Social Security of all newly registered addicts between 1968 and 1970 revealed that only 42 percent had ever been found guilty of any criminal offense either as an adult or a juvenile. Of these, most were for sale or use of illegal drugs. By contrast, a New York City study of 416 addicts indicated that 84 percent had been arrested at least once, averaging two-thirds of a charge per person for every year of their addiction. Property offenses actually outnumbered drug offenses for this sample.[39]

Obviously this comparison is only suggestive. Neither arrests nor convictions are an accurate index of criminality, and the comparison of different indexes for the same criteria is inappropriate. Nevertheless, a certain magnitude of difference is clearly apparent.

If there is little or no interdependence of the criminal and drug subcultures in England, it seems reasonable that juvenile drug experimenters would be little inclined toward engaging in nondrug related forms of crime. A study sponsored by the Ciba Foundation concluded that "delinquency among [British] juvenile drug takers is apparently disproportionately high *only* for crimes directly concerned with procuring drugs."[40]

In the same year, a study was made of the addicts in London's prisons. It was found that three-quarters had a history of court convictions predating their addiction to narcotics—a situation that appears to exist in the United States, which will be covered more fully later. Unfortunately, no breakdown was given on offense categories. Furthermore, the author goes on to draw the rather unlikely conclusion that his prison sample is quite representative of the British addict.[41]

Another interesting study was undertaken recently in which the criminal careers of the *same* group of addicts were studied as they lived in different environments. Canada has a control system almost identical to that of the United States; during the 1960s 91 Canadian addicts were known to have migrated to England. Twenty-five of these addicts were located with the following results: "At home, the Canadians spent 25% of their addicted years . . . in jail; in England, less than 2%. . . ." During the same period, they compiled 88 theft offenses at home, and 8 in England.[42]

These results suggest that Canadian addicts are essentially noncriminal addicts, and that drug maintenance has allowed them to return to a conventional life-style. The argument continues that since Canadian and American addicts are similar, much of our crime problem could be solved with a similar policy of drug maintenance. Unfortunately, there are two serious and possibly fatal defects in the above study, and therefore, with any inferences drawn from it. First, the fact that almost two-thirds (66) of the original sample disappeared is hardly justification for assuming that the remaining 25 were representative of even that sample. Second, there are a number of reasons to suspect that those 91 addicts were not at all representative of the picture in Canada. The very fact that they moved is highly unusual for addicts. Their almost complete lack of geographical mobility has been thoroughly documented.[43]

In sum, there are both addicts and criminals in Britain, and the combination of the two, especially when it involves property offenses, is far rarer than in this country. There is no need or economic basis for extended contact between the two; hence, none exists. A 1970 Scotland Yard report stated bluntly: "There is no concrete evidence to connect any particular criminal activity with those dependent on the 'hard' drugs [viz., the opiates]. . . .''

The Economics of Heroin and the Impact of Law Enforcement in the United States

A detailed analysis here of the economics of heroin would be both inappropriate and unwieldy. Nevertheless, it is worthwhile to note that the economic impact of addiction extends beyond the usual calculations of enforcement costs and property losses from addict crimes to such areas as: supplemental income in the form of police bribes, profits from resale of confiscated drugs, public outcry for increased budgets for the police, production of methadone and other opiate antagonists, real estate profits from development of rehabilitation centers, social scientists' competition for research money, and even the sale of "clean" urine.[44]

Actual drug costs, however, are the principal concern here. Printed estimates of drug costs vary erratically, depending upon the point the author is trying to make. For example, a 1969 article in the D.C. *Medical Annals* stated that Washington addicts were spending between $50 and $150 per day for their habit. Furthermore, nearly all of this amount was the proceeds of crime. The fact is that the mean daily cost of supporting a heroin habit during that year was about $18 per day (source: BNDD).

Consider for a moment the apparent consensus in this country that most addicts were criminals prior to their addiction. The question then becomes how much of that $18 would not have been stolen were it not for the narcotics habit. A thief of rather average ability would be likely to raise at least that amount on a daily basis whether or not he was addicted. Since most addict-thieves deal in drugs on the side, this becomes an additional source of income. Furthermore, drug costs were not always that high. Although the $1 per day habit of the 1920s is distant history, it is only recently that street opiates have become extremely expensive. In 1955, for example, only one year before the Senate subcommittee (infra.) concluded that one-half of all urban crime was the result of drug addiction, Commissioner Harry Anslinger testified that mean drug costs were $10 nationally and only $8 a day in New York City. Prior to 1969, the belief that addiction substantially increased reported crime is at least open to question.

Law enforcement policy on drug seizures is rather simple: the more the better. It is reasoned that fewer drugs reaching the street will mean that fewer people will experiment with them. Many of those already addicted will be forced to give up the habit because of the shortage. Those not addicted will find it very difficult to purchase drugs for three reasons: (1) They are more suspect because they are not well-known addicts; (2) the shortage will mean that dealers will be more pressured to service only steady customers; and (3) prices will rise sufficiently high that experimenters will be deterred.

The available data on the effectiveness of this policy show some rather interesting trends. Seizures of heroin have increased almost 300 percent since 1969. Mean daily drug costs have risen in the same period (1969 through 1972) from \$18 to \$48; and the estimated number of addicts has also risen from 315,000 to 626,000—almost double (all data: BNDD). Since the same agency is using the same procedure over time, it is reasonable to conclude that any errors in estimating will be a constant bias not affecting relative changes. Evidently, if any relationship does exist between opiate costs and the extent of opiate addiction, it is not an inverse one.

Furthermore, there appears to be a disturbing and unintended consequence of efficient enforcement. It was argued earlier that \$18 was an expensive but not altogether exorbitant daily drug cost. Little, if any, *additional* crime would be needed to meet such an expense. This argument begins to lose merit, however, as that cost increases. At \$50 a day—the current mean—the addict requires over \$17,000 per year for drugs alone.

Is it possible that our control efforts have created the very problem that they were designed to suppress? A recent conference in New Delhi on narcotic addiction came to the following conclusions with respect to that issue:

1. Drug addiction does not seem to be connected with crime except where there is legislation to prohibit nonmedical use.

2. Efforts to control addiction probably will not reduce the number of addicts but may increase the amount of crime.[45]

There is a considerable difference between addicts whose thefts net them \$20 or \$30 per day versus \$70 or \$80 per day. While some would operate in that upper range regardless of their addiction, there are, no doubt, others, particularly the new addicts who become "locked into" a life-style of confirmed criminal activity as the price climbs. In short, I suggest that we may be witnessing a disquieting paradox in social control: that more effective law enforcement has created more street crime.

Careers and Criminal Careers of Addicts

To delineate the outlines of a likely career for the criminal addict provides a useful aid in understanding the developing relationship between addiction and crime. This type of process puts significant events both in sequence and in context. Published literature suggests something like the following.[a]

The future addict begins experimentation with opiates (usually heroin) at an early age, probably between 15 and 18. Addiction (daily use) generally follows within several months. Many, of course, experiment but do not become addicted.[b] The youth most likely to be involved is an inner city black male. He has probably been picked up by the police at least once for less serious offenses such as truancy, gambling, joyriding, and vandalism. Some of his friends, however, have been involved in more serious crimes. As opiate use intensifies, the youth's circle of friends narrows to include mostly other drug users. While earlier behavior did involve some criminal offenses, most of his behavior could be described as conventional. Now the costs of daily use are very different from the costs of experimentation. Crime becomes a more earnest enterprise and is more oriented toward gainful offenses such as burglary and larceny. The addict's dependence upon criminal friends is almost complete: they not only continue his training as a thief but through them operates the informal grapevine on police activities and drug sources.

The addict, now in his early twenties, has probably been arrested several times (2-6). Diversion to treatment programs has not worked

---

[a] This is a somewhat impressionistic composite drawn from such authors as The Shafer Commission, The Hayim Report, Edwin Schur, R. Battegay, B. Brown, and others found in the bibliography.

[b] Indications are that only one in six or seven actually becomes addicted. That determination will not be a part of this study.

well. Even methadone has done little but allow the addict more freedom in the way he spends the money from his crimes. At this intermediate stage in his career, the addict may be described as a criminal who happens to be using an opiate drug. For the most part, narcotic expenses seem to be deducted from the profits of an ongoing pattern of illicit activity. Of course, to some extent, the nature and regularity of this pattern is influenced by the recurring need to purchase drugs. While this is not a problem for most addicts, for some, their habits get "out of hand." It is no longer a deductible expense. Some intensify crime as a response to this while others seek treatment, a situation which allows the habit to be resumed later at a nominal cost.

Age ultimately has its impact. As the addict reaches his late twenties or early thirties the life of the street and the constant hustle over the years becomes less attractive. Few street addicts reach middle age without experiencing overdoses, septicemia, or hepatitis. This is a time in which the addict is more vulnerable to change. The "older" addict is more likely to respond to treatment—including methadone—than his younger counterparts.

Although this scenario seems to be the most common, others do exist. These possible variations are presented in the next section as a developmental typology of addiction.

The Framework

An analytically useful means of examining the link between addiction and crime at both individual and aggregate levels may be found by observing developmental differences among addicts at similar points in time. Presumably an examination of the forces at work at the points of critical dissimilarities would yield some greater understanding of the place of crime in the addict career track. Accordingly, the following logical typology with associated sequences is suggested to constitute the likely range of interrelationships for addiction and crime in this culture. This typology will be of considerable aid in the later analysis and discussion of data. The reader may wish to note that sequences A, D, and E (outlined below) will turn out to be of relatively greater importance and utility than the others.

The Naive Addict (Sequence A)

1. Generally legitimate activity (possible minor delinquency)
2. Drug experimentation
3. Opiate addiction
4. Crime to support the habit
5. Remission: either abstinence or drug maintenance
6. Significant reduction in crime

It is suggested later that the naive addict is less common than is widely believed. Nevertheless, the fact that some essentially noncriminal people are forced into a criminal life-style to support an expensive habit does raise some serious questions about our social policy.

The Legitimate Junkie (Sequence B)

1. Generally legitimate activity (possible minor delinquency)
2. Drug experimentation
3. Opiate addiction
4. No increase in delinquent activity except as directly related to drug acquisition
5. Remission
6. No activity change

The legitimate junkies are usually medical doctors, pharmacists, nurses, and other noncriminal addicts with legal or quasi-legal access to drugs. Their life-style in almost every respect is vastly different from the street addict. Very little is known about the physician addict, for example, and yet it is estimated that at least 1 in every 100 doctors is an addict.[46]

The Medical Addict (Sequence C)

1. Generally legitimate activity (possible minor delinquency)
2. Therapeutic opiate use
3. Opiate addiction

4. No increase in delinquent activity; drugs are legally available
5. Remission
6. No activity change

A proportionately rather small number of people become addicted while receiving therapeutic doses. Relapse following withdrawal is unusual, and this addict poses no significant medical or social problem.

The Criminal Addict–Marginal (Sequence D)

1. Moderate criminal activity
2. Drug experimentation
3. Opiate addiction
4. Continued or slightly intensified criminal activity
5. Remission
6. Slightly reduced criminal activity

The marginal criminal addicts are victims of social policy. From the urban slums, the source of 80 percent of our addicts,[47] there are many who drift into delinquency.[48] While many drift out as they age, those who become addicted have little choice. There are few who can afford a mean yearly drug cost of $17,000 on a conventional salary (BNDD estimate, March 1973).

The Criminal Addict–Confirmed (Sequence E)

1. Extensive criminal activity
2. Drug experimentation
3. Opiate addiction
4. Continued criminal activity
5. Remission
6. Continued criminal activity with no change

Millions of dollars have been spent in the belief that the confirmed addict would give up crime when freed of his habit. Data indicate, however, that there is little relationship between his habit and his criminal activity. Very early and extensive involvement in the criminal subculture has effectively precluded integration into a conventional life-style. As one methadone maintained prostitute put it, "The only thing I'm good enough at is boosting and turning tricks."[49]

The Old Man (Sequence F)

1. Moderate to extensive criminal activity
2. Drug experimentation
3. Opiate addiction
4. Continued or intensified criminal activity
5. Cure
6. Significant reduction in crime

Quite probably, "the old man" is the rarest category. The mortality rate for addicts is over 15 times the equivalent age group in the general population;[50] many are serving long sentences for felony convictions; and many have "matured out" of their addiction.[51] The older addict has consistently shown more improvement during treatment than his younger peers. This clearly seems to be an artifact of age and the life-style of addiction rather than the method of treatment.

Sequences B and C are included only for completeness. What is known about both indicates they have little relevance for this study.

Preaddictive Criminality

In terms of developmental patterns, the critical distinction between sequences A (naive addict), D (marginal criminal), and E (confirmed criminal) is the incidence of criminal activity prior to addiction. Sequence A (naive addict), for example, is widely believed to be the modal career track for addicts. David Maurer and Victor Vogel tell us that "[a]s soon as the addict finds the means . . . of raising the large amounts of money necessary to support his increasing habit, he becomes a criminal."[52] Evidently, preaddictive crime is either ignored as irrelevant or assumed not to exist.

The Shafer Commission, on the other hand, seems to feel that other sequences are more likely:

The available data indicate that most known opiate (primarily heroin) dependent persons had long histories of delinquent or criminal behavior prior to their being identified as drug users, that opiate use becomes a further expression of delinquent tendencies, and that most heroin-dependent persons continue to be arrested subsequent to release from prisons, hospitals, or treatment.[53]

Data from several studies are reviewed briefly to show that many addicts were, in fact, involved in crime prior to addiction; self-reporting studies would indicate an even higher proportion if the facts were known.

Cross-cultural data on this subject are quite rare. One recent study of 90 addict-prisoners in Japan showed that 88 admitted engaging in a "variety of delinquent acts" prior to becoming addicted. Since the Japanese government has modeled its drug control policies after the United States, the findings are of some interest. Unfortunately, the sample that was chosen cannot be considered representative.[54]

A 1965 New York study showed that "a majority" of the addicts had criminal records prior to the beginning of opiate use. The author concludes that "addiction is not a cause of crime but a product of delinquent lives."[55]

Examination of the rap sheets of addicts admitted in 1965 to the California Rehabilitation Center shows that only 5 percent were without earlier recorded criminal activity.[56]

In 1963 a more extensive study was done in California of 7,932 arrested addicts, none of whom had prior drug records. The breakdown of criminal activity prior to the first arrest for drugs is shown in table 1-1.[57] By inspection it can be seen that two-thirds of this large sample *appeared* to be involved in crime before addiction, some more than others. The problem is that in each case arrests are used as a proxy for the activity in question. One has to make the assumption that the time lag between activity and arrest is reasonably constant. If it is not, then the apparent temporal sequence may be invalid.

G. E. Vaillant and L. J. Brill did a 12-year follow-up of 100 New York City addicts. Although many began drug use before age 18, "at least 57% of our group were antisocial (chronically truant, dishonorably discharged or in reform school) *prior* to the use of drugs. . . ."[58]

Table 1-1

Criminal Activity Prior to First Drug Arrest, California, 1963

No previous police record	32.6%
Minor police record	43.4%
More than one felony charge	18.2%
Served time in prison	5.8%
	100.0%

Note: N = 7,932.

Source: Maurer and Vogel 1970.

In another study on addiction and crime, John O'Donnell states that 63 percent of the men in his sample (266) had no arrests prior to addiction. More importantly, he finds a powerful association between the year of addiction and crime before addiction (see table 1-2). In addition, an inverse relationship between the age at which addiction began and the frequency of crimes prior to addiction was discovered; or in other words, "the younger a man was at the onset of addiction, the more likely he was to have committed criminal acts before addiction."[59] This finding has been verified by the Law Enforcement Assistance Administration (LEAA) funded study of methadone maintained addicts in New York City.[60]

Given what is known about the shifting age of present addicts, we can infer that the addict profile also remains in transition. The mean age at the onset of addiction has been declining for years. In addition, addicts appear to be recruited more frequently from criminal ranks. The addict subculture appears to be in almost complete dependence upon criminal associations for both support and technology. Since the age at addiction is still declining, the new addicts have even less opportunity than their predecessors of returning to a conventional life-style—a life-style they scarcely knew.

Table 1-3 is a rather indirect but interesting indication of that relationship. It shows that as the source of narcotics becomes increasingly illegal, the user becomes increasingly likely to be arrested, convicted, and sentenced for a crime.[61]

Except, perhaps, for those with quasi-legitimate access to narcotics, most of these people probably had trouble with the law prior to their addiction. Given the relative demographic homogeneity of the street addict in this country, there is reason to believe, based on self-reporting studies, that the true incidence of

Table 1-2
Crime and the Year of Addiction, Lexington, Kentucky Sample

Year of Addiction	N	No Crime Before Addiction (percent)
Before 1920	20	95
1920-29	35	77
1930-39	62	65
1940-49	60	62
1950-59	19	53
Total	196	

Source: O'Donnell 1966 Table 2, p. 378. © *Social Probelems* 13:4 (Spring 1966). Reprinted by permission of *Social Problems*, the Society for the Study of Social Problems, and John A. O'Donnell.

Table 1-3
Narcotics Source and Postaddiction Sentencing, Lexington, Kentucky Sample

Source of Narcotics	N	Percentage Never Sentenced After Addiction
Doctors only, one at a time	45	91
Several doctors, and/or exempt narcotics	22	77
Mainly own supply	12	75
Some medical, some illegal	29	62
Mostly or all illegal	82	28
Total	190	

Note: Several men could not be classified on sources of narcotics.

Source: O'Donnell 1966 Table 3, p. 381. © *Social Problems* 13:4 (Spring 1966). Reprinted by permission of *Social Problems*, the Society for the Study of Social Problems, and John A. O'Donnell.

criminal activity prior to addiction is quite high.[62] Preliminary results of the New York City study [63] show that "official charges understate the amounts of illegal behavior committed by the sample."

A study of 90 addicts certified to the Narcotics Addiction Control Commission (NACC) revealed that although 100 percent of the males admitted extensive criminal activity, only 79 percent had ever been arrested. The data also suggest that only one crime was cleared by arrest for every 120 offenses committed by the addicts in the sample.[64]

The issues of age, life-style, and frequency of criminal behavior prior to addiction are all related. There is no certainty that any juvenile is either a marginal (sequence D) or a confirmed (sequence E) criminal. Most ghetto juveniles grow up in a twilight zone where conventional and criminal behavior patterns seem to coexist. Heroin seems to change all that. "Whereas the juvenile delinquent often drifts out of his gang to work and raise a family, the addict becomes enmeshed in the drug subculture, where 'hustling' and arrests are common and in which steady employment and normal family life are impossible."[65]

Criminal Behavior During Addiction and the Impact of Intervention

The LEAA funded New York City study is clearly the most sophisticated attempt to look at, among other things, some of the issues of addiction and crime.[66] Their sample consists of 416 methadone maintained addicts, all of whom were volunteers over the age of 21. Mean entry age into their program is 33 compared with 26 for the New York register. Most had been addicted since the age of 21, and 84 percent had been arrested at least once, most many times. Each addict averaged 0.65 charges for every year of his addiction. This figure peaked, however, at 1.03 charges in the year preceding entry into the program. They suggest that these figures are "not . . . higher than the crime rates of addicts in the general population."

Although it is obvious that nearly all of the addicts considered in table 1-4[c] engaged in crime during their addiction, only one-half listed it as the *primary* source of income.

There is a tendency for street addicts to escalate the seriousness of their offenses as their addiction continues. In the New York

[c] The data in tables 1-4, 1-5, and 1-6 is drawn from Hayim, Gila et al., 1973. *Heroin Use and Crime in a Methadone Maintenance Program: An Interim Report*, U.S. Department of Justice, Law Enforcement Assistance Administration. Washington: U.S. Government Printing Office. The fact that the National Institute of Law Enforcement and Criminal Justice furnished financial support to the activities described in this publication does not necessarily indicate the concurrence of the Institute in the statements or conclusions contained herein.

Table 1-4
Primary Source of Addict Income for a Sample of New York Methadone Maintained Addicts

Legitimate job	18%
Welfare	19%
Spouse-Kin	7%
Other or unknown	8%
Illegal	48%

Note: $N = 416$.

Source: Hayim 1973. Reprinted by permission.

study, property offenses averaged 0.07 charges per person-year before addiction. This was, incidentally, the most frequent charge during that period. During addiction it rose to 0.20, and in the year preceding treatment it reached 0.26. Only one other category—drug offenses (sale and possession)—showed any significant change. Those rates were 0.02, 0.24, and 0.45 respectively.

Although the mean daily cost for addicts in New York during 1972 was about $40 or $45, these addicts had been using heroin for an average of 12 years. Their daily minimum cost was about $75.[67] The rapid rise in drug offenses is another indication that their habits were "out of hand."

These addicts do, in fact, steal to support the habit. They are the targets of those who advocate drug maintenance as a solution to rising property crime. Some of their claims are considered first, followed by an indication of which have a factual basis and which are wishful thinking.[d]

The 1972 Canadian Le Dain Commission, in discussing methadone maintenance, states that "the foremost expectation is that all patients who are treated will become law-abiding citizens. . . ." Erich Goode puts it more bluntly: "Methadone gets the addict out of the way . . . and reduces his crime rate dramatically."[68]

The proponents of methadone maintenance do not hesitate to indicate how much crime will be reduced by their program. A 1969 editorial in *Modern Medicine* urges support for further study and development of methadone programs. The author cites average reductions of 90 percent in criminal convictions as proof of suc-

[d] Consideration of treatment modalities other than methadone maintenance will not be attempted by this research.

cess.[69] The beliefs of Drs. Vincent P. Dole and Marie E. Nyswander, early advocates of methadone, are perhaps the most spectacular and well-known. After a four-year trial, they claim a 94 percent reduction in the criminal activity of 750 former heroin addicts.[70]

Recent claims seem to be more conservative, even skeptical. The proceedings of the third National Conference on Methadone state that "it is difficult to find any hard data" to support the claims of greatly decreased criminality and greatly increased employment.[71]

Many claims are founded on a rather inartful manipulation of the data. The following excerpt from a recent article is an example:

Ninety-four (10.5%) of the 900 patients admitted to the program were rearrested for 101 crimes committed over the 34-month treatment period. Some patients were rearrested on more than one charge. . . . For the 4-year period prior to admission to methadone treatment the patients amassed a minimum of 900 arrests. . . .[72]

The conclusion is, of course, that there were 799 fewer arrests because of methadone. There are several problems with this conclusion. It is inappropriate to use periods of grossly different lengths (34 v. 48 months) when it is obvious that arrests are a function of time. Also, the exclusive use of the years immediately preceding treatment for comparison purposes tends to be misleading, since this is normally the time of the most intense criminal activity. Finally, the sample consisted of probationers. Regardless of any rehabilitative efforts, those who are convicted and then given probation may be less likely as an aggregate to commit as many crimes as before their arrest.

The New York study[73] shows some results that are quite different from the usual claims. Note the changes in rates shown in table 1-5. There was actually an insignificant increase in the number of charges in all but one of the categories after one year in the program.

Although not specifically stated as such, there appear to be two factors that influence the results of the New York study: (1) prior criminality, and (2) age.

1. By the end of 24 months, one-third of the 416 had dropped out of the program. The criminal activity of this group was significantly higher both during and after treatment than those who remained in the program. Furthermore, "terminated patients had higher rates of arrests *prior* to their entering treatment than did patients who remained in treatment, pointing to the fact that those who are retained

Table 1-5

Rate of Charges Per Person/Year for a Sample of New York Methadone Maintained Addicts

Type of Police Charges	During Addiction	One Year After Program Entry
Drug offenses	0.24	0.36
Property offenses	0.20	0.21
Assault	0.04	0.09
Property-Assault	0.01	0.02
Prostitution	0.03	0.04
Forgery	0.05	0.01

Note: $N = 416$.

Source: Hayim 1973. Reprinted by permission.

tend to be less 'criminal' to begin with."[74] The extensive criminal activity of addicts who do not do well in treatment programs has been documented previously. A Canadian study concluded that addicts admitted for treatment more than once prior to the three-year study were quicker to relapse and had much higher rates of criminal activity, particularly property offenses.[75] There is no mystery here. Except for those who are either civilly or criminally committed, there is a continuous process of self-selection for those who seek treatment. Those who never seek it or do so without commitment seem to be more heavily involved in property crime and may well be, for the most part, "confirmed" criminals (sequence E). But this observation must be qualified by the considerations of age.

2. The influence of age appeared in two manners. It was found that age at the onset of addiction was a rather good predictor of criminality during treatment. The earlier the onset of addiction, the less likely the addict was to relinquish his criminal life-style during treatment. This finding is consistent with the observations of O'Donnell cited previously. Those who became addicted very early encountered the most difficulty in adjusting to a conventional life-style that they actually never knew.

The second effect of age is really a corollary of the first. Younger patients, who also were addicted earlier, fared considerably worse than the older ones, both in terms of absolute numbers and relative changes. Table 1-6 illustrates some of the differences.[76]

Table 1-6

Crime Rate Differences Based on Charges Per Person/Year One Year Before and After Program Entry for a Sample of New York Methadone Maintained Addicts

Charges	Age Groupings			
	21-25	26-30	31-34	35+
Before program entry	0.46	0.23	0.26	0.20
Property	+0.06	+0.08	−0.12	−0.09
After program entry	0.52	0.31	0.14	0.11
Before program entry	0.00	0.02	0.03	0.00
Robbery	+0.05	+0.01	−0.03	0.00
After program entry	0.05	0.03	0.00	0.00
	(N = 58)	(N = 98)	(N = 73)	(N = 187)

Source: Modified from Hayim 1973. Used with permission.

Perhaps the most significant item about this table is the fact that Hayim used the year preceding entry as the baseline for comparison. This year, by the addicts' own estimates, is the time of most intensive criminal activity. By inspection it can be seen that the gainful, "street-type" offenses actually increased for the addicts under 30, even though they had been relieved of any expense for maintaining the habit. No explanation is offered by the author for this.

Earlier in this work it was suggested that two types of criminal addict exist: marginal and confirmed. It also was suggested that the marginal criminal would show considerably more improvement than the other type. Evidently, most of those addicts between ages 21 and 30 were confirmed criminals and continue to be so. What is not known is how many of them made a transition from marginal to confirmed as the length of their addiction progressed. It seems reasonable to conclude that the forced and protracted interdependence of the addict and criminal subcultures would have a long-term criminogenic effect on its members.

In other words, by our control policies on opiate drugs, we have placed many marginal addicts in a position in which it is almost certain that they will become confirmed criminals—if they were not already. The need for heroin coupled with the lack of any legitimate sources makes a conventional life-style for the new addict all but impossible. Gainful stealing then originates in need but continues as a way of life. It is not surprising, therefore, that the sudden substitution of a free opiate for an expensive one makes very little change in the way the addict relates to an environment that otherwise has not changed.

It might seem that early intervention would be the most successful. It has, in fact, been the least successful. Although the new addict's habit is rather inexpensive, and he may not yet be deeply involved in crime, he is still on "the honeymoon." At this early stage the drug seems like a solution to any problem; there have been few if any arrests, bummers, hot shots, panics, and O.D.'s. In short, there is little stress to provide any motivation to change.[e]

Why then the gradual downtrend in street crime for the addicts over 30? For them the honeymoon is in the distant past. The most useful way of looking at their situation is to consider them as criminals who happen to be addicted to an opiate drug. It is well-known that a correlation exists between age and crime.[77] For whatever the reasons, as the criminal reaches his late twenties, there is a rather general and steady decrease in his illicit activities. There is no reason to believe that this process does not operate equally well for the criminal addict—with one exception: Although he may have reached the age during which most criminals "mature out'" the fact of addiction keeps the older addict thoroughly locked into his lifestyle. For him the substitution of a free opiate for an expensive one is significant.

Literature Summary

Although the literature is contradictory on many of the specific points linking addiction and crime, several areas of consensus are present.

It is clear, for example, that a widespread belief exists that narcotic addicts are responsible for an enormous amount of property crime as a result of opiate addiction. The mechanism linking these two is not well-defined and is frequently not even questioned. Cross-cultural, medical, and historical literature provide a rather mixed picture, but one which indicates that extensive opiate use is

[e] Most of the ideas in this paragraph were those of Judge Lawrence Pierce, former Commissioner of the New York Narcotic Addiction Control Commssission.

not necessarily accompanied by extensive crime. In the United States, recognition of the complexity of the problem is growing. Several observers have noted the extensive involvement of many addicts in crime prior to their addiction. Unfortunately, the nature and extent of this activity is usually poorly documented. There also is little or no recognition of the impact of drug control policies on the recruitment patterns affecting these addicts.

The literature offers a variety of estimates on the economic costs of addict crime. These estimates tend to vary erratically and rarely address themselves to such issues as how much of that amount would have been stolen had the involved group not been addicted to an opiate. Another economic issue not addressed in the literature is which of several alternatives does the addict tend to select when faced with sharply increased drug costs.

The response of the addict to treatment is perhaps the most well-documented segment of the literature on addiction and crime. In spite of some earlier reports, there appears to be a growing consensus that treatment—including drug maintenance—has only a modest impact on the nature and volume of crime committed by the addict-patients. Age appears in the literature as a potentially significant factor in two areas: the younger the addict at addiction onset, the more likely it is that he will become involved in extensive crime; the older the addict at treatment, the more likely it is that he will be able to readjust to a conventional life-style.

Generally, the literature on addiction and crime is suggestive but rarely conclusive. In many cases, findings are stated about some specific aspect of the relationship without the necessary attempt to integrate the findings into a comprehensive explanatory system.

2

The Addicts

Descriptions of people and places can be both factual and impersonal or subjective and anecdotal. Each of these is appropriate here. A brief discussion of the interview settings with some of the problems encountered there is followed by a review of selected personal and demographic characteristics of the interview sample. Some of these more critical characteristics are then compared with similar items from a nationwide survey. Finally, a few personal profiles of the addicts themselves are offered. Without elaboration, machine printouts seem devoid of the very hmanity that is under study.

Interview Sites

Initially two and then later three locations were selected as interview sites. All of these locations are in predominantly black, deteriorated sectors of the city known to have a high proportion of addicts. Two locations are classified by the Narcotics Treatment Administration (NTA) as "outpatient clinics" and the other as an "inpatient clinic"—a locked ward on the top floor of D.C. General Hospital. The locked ward is reserved for "clients," as they are called, who are either under physical restraint by court order, have voluntarily opted for detoxification from either heroin or methadone, or have some complications requiring medical observation.

The outpatient clinics are strictly walk-in. The addicts come every day except Sunday to receive either maintenance or gradual detoxification doses of methadone from the clinic in which they are registered. Each is assigned a counselor. A typical visit consists of some "counseling" and a trip to a bulletproof window facing out from a separate, locked compartment, not unlike the arrangement in many banks. Here the addict receives a preset quantity of methadone or "meth"—usually between 30 and 60 milligrams—mixed with Tang in a medicine cup. The large blockage doses of over 100 milligrams that were once popular are now rarely used.

27

Withdrawal was very difficult and euphoria was common at such levels.

Cooperation was clearly the most serious concern. In spite of a phone call from the director of NTA research to each of the clinics explaining both the nature and confidentiality of the interviews, initially I was met with considerable suspicion and hostility from the staff. There is, as the director observed, no great groundswell of support for outside researchers. Being Caucasian in a black-operated clinic doing research on black addicts was still another problem. One of the clinics refused me any interviews until a meeting of the entire staff was called, during which it was my task to explain in detail what I wanted and why I wanted it. In what developed as a lengthy cross-examination, I was told, among other things, that no one would talk to me. Nevertheless, since the interviews were authorized, I was allowed to begin.

Client Cooperation

The initial hostility was not long-lived. Interviewing began in late December and continued into May 1974. During this time the pattern of hostility gradually evolved into one of limited cooperation or, at the worst, neutrality. In some cases, counselors would even suggest to their clients that they participate.

Client cooperation was to remain, however, a chronic problem. Most of the addicts were not referred by any counselor and had to be approached directly for their consent. Approximately a third of these agreed to the interview. The rest had a broad range of excuses.

All respondents were first read and then given a "Statement of Purpose" form prior to the interview (see appendix A.). Although confidentiality and anonymity were explicitly promised, a few remained very suspicious. Pee Wee was an extreme case representative of this problem. I first began to interview him in January. After only a few minutes of shifting in his chair and answering evasively, Pee Wee blurted out: "That piece of paper says I don't have to say nothin', right?"

"Right."

"Well, I don't feel like sayin' nothin'."

I saw Pee Wee again in March, but again he declined to participate. Finally, in May, he consented to a lengthy interview that outlined, among other things, a continuing pattern of armed robberies.

Toward the end of April, I began using an attractive female companion to interview with me. I had noticed earlier that female addicts seemed more amenable to spending 30 to 40 minutes with a male interviewer than did their male counterparts. Following this observation, respondents were interviewed by a member of the opposite sex whenever possible. Unfortunately, this discovery was not made until late in the stage of data collecting.

Small things seemed to influence the likelihood of obtaining interviews. Mornings were the least productive. I once waited three hours without a successful contact. Those addicts that did come to the facilities in the morning were nearly always taking work breaks or were otherwise occupied. Mondays generally provided fewer successful contacts. Since the clinics are closed on Sunday, the clients are given an extra dose of methadone for that day. However, some admit shooting or selling that dose on Saturday. The signs of early withdrawal are written on the faces of many standing at the clinic window on Monday. These people do not want to talk to anyone. Urine days were also a problem. The periodic and unannounced use of urine surveillance frequently resulted in nasty disputes between counselors and clients who were anxious to avoid another "dirty urine" in their files. At that moment, it was very difficult to impress those addicts with the need for more quality research on drug addiction.

Client Profile

The sample interviewed represented a considerable age range from 17 to 56 with a mean of 27. Most of the respondents were male (70 percent) and black (89 percent). While many admitted early use of other drugs, particularly alcohol and marijuana, initial use of opiates began on the average at age 19 (median 18.2, std. dev. 4.1). It is important to note that heroin was in almost every case the first (91 percent) and most consistently used opiate. Six percent reported cough syrup (codeine) as the first opiate abused while morphine, methadone, and demerol were mentioned only once.

A rather surprising finding was that the majority of respondents (56 percent) reported "snorting" as the initial method of use.

Snorting is much like the name implies. A "cap" or "bag" is broken into small mounds on a plain piece of paper. Each small mound of powder is about half the area of the nail on a man's little finger. The mound is then quickly inhaled through the open nostril - the other being pinched shut. Although the effect is almost instantaneous, addicts uniformly agree that it is wasteful. A few, however, never do graduate to "the spike." One was so proud of that fact that she made a point of showing her arms to the interviewer. Snorting is of interest for another reason. Addicts seem to hold many misconceptions about the very drugs they are using. One of the more popular ones is that snorting either produces no habit or a very small and, therefore, manageable one. Unfortunately, quite the opposite is true. Once a habit begins to develop, the switch to the spike is usually made in the name of economy.

Quite a few addicts (25 percent) bypass the early stages of snorting and "oil" or "mainline" from the beginning. The other two alternatives are "skinpopping" (subcutaneous injection—12 percent) and ingestion (7 percent). This latter method is only for cough syrup and tablets; heroin cannot be taken orally.

For the most part, sample members were not geographically mobile. Seventy-four percent indicated that they had never lived outside the Washington metropolitan area. A few (5 percent) were quite mobile and reported living in five or more cities after acquiring a habit.

Three-fourths of the sample did not finish high school. Educational levels ranged from the fifth grade to two years of college with an average of ten and one-half years. The modal age for leaving school was 16. Generally, the use of opiates began after dropping out of school (71 percent). Of those that began while still in school, a slight majority (52 percent) stated that it did *not* influence their decision to quit school.

All of the clinics accept both court referrals and volunteers; the latter category accounts for 79 percent of this sample. A majority of the clients (56 percent) were on gradual detoxification; the next largest category was maintenance (23 percent). Prior to registering with NTA, the addicts averaged 4.9 years of street opiate use.

Since this sample is actually a nonrandom subsample of the entire (2,400) NTA population, it is important to verify that it is reasonably representative of that population. Note the comparisons on these four variables in table 2-1. These inconsequential differ-

Table 2-1
**Selected Comparisons of Sample with the Entire Population of the
Narcotics Treatment Administration**

	Interview Sample	NTA Population
Mean age	27	26
Male-Female ratio	70-30	70-30
Black-White ratio	89-11	93- 7
Volunteer-Court referral ratio	79-21	75-25
	(N = 101)	(N = 2,400)

ences suggest that the cooperating addicts were quite similar to the larger population on several important variables.

The status of the respondent as either volunteer or referred by court offers another possibility for assessing the representativeness of the research sample. Since this undertaking places considerable emphasis on the factors affecting variations in criminal life-style orientation, it is important to learn whether the selection process itself has any consequences for that orientation. For example, do addicts referred by the court tend to engage in serious crime more often than volunteers? Or, does the selection process seem irrelevant to the pattern of criminal activity? The impact of this selection process is evaluated in table 2-2.

Not surprisingly, the corrected chi square for this table is nearly zero (0.1). It appears that motivation for treatment has no predictable implications for the degree of criminal involvement. This finding suggests that the addicts interviewed from this sample may not be materially different in terms of criminal orientation from those not currently visible to official agencies.

Comparative information on a national level would allow generalizations from this sample to be made with greater confidence. There is, of course, no information to suggest that Washington addicts behave in a manner characteristic of addicts nationally. Nevertheless, demonstration of some basic similarities would indicate that cautious generalizations would not be unreasonable. In 1973, 192 interviewers from The Johns Hopkins School of Hygiene and Public Health interviewed 1,328 addicts in treatment in the nation's 31 largest cities. Some of the comparable data are listed

Table 2-2
Addicts' Program Status by Dichotomous Indexes of Criminality
(Marginal and Confirmed)

	Program Status		
Type of Criminality	Volunteer	Court Referral	Row Total
Frequency	53	16	
Confirmed			69
(Expected value)	(54)	(16)	
Frequency	25	7	
Marginal–includes naive			32
(Expected value)	(25)	(7)	
Total	78	23	101

Note: $N = 101$.

in table 2-3. Except for the very high concentration of blacks, Washington's addicts appear to be quite average.

The literature on heroin addicts is replete with generalizations about their passive-dependent nature, their high prevalence of psychosis, their extensive involvement in crime, etc. While these and other traits were present in some and not in others, there appear to be few if any identifiable clusters of characteristics that could not be found among urban ghetto dwellers generally. The single habit shared by all was addiction to an opiate—and that opiate was in almost every case heroin. The brief vignettes that follow describe the range of their personal beliefs, social habits, and criminal careers.

The Interviews

Ebony was an attractive black woman of 24. She began her habit at the age of 20 when a friend showed her how to "cold shake" dolophine tablets in a syringe. Ironically, dolophine is an opiate that is used almost exclusively to withdraw heroin addicts. Ebony was somewhat unique in that Washington was the fifth city she had lived in during the previous four years. The extensive involvement with crime that forced these moves did not begin with drugs. As a

Table 2-3

Selected Comparisons of Narcotics Treatment Administration Sample with Nationwide Survey Data Obtained from 31 Cities

	Washington Interview Sample	Nationwide Survey
Mean age	27	27
Male-Female ratio	70-30	80-20
Black-White ratio	89-11	66-34
Mean educational level	10.5	10.8
Median age at first use	18.3	18.6
	(N = 101)	(N = 1,328)

teenager, Ebony was constantly involved with auto theft and shoplifting, and to a lesser extent with robbery and carrying weapons. Although only 24, she admits having 15 arrests: robbery 3, larceny 7, possession 2, forgery 2, and narcotics vagrancy 1. Ebony worked with a stick-up gang in New York for a while until her ulcer began to grow severe. She then moved to Detroit and obtained a job as a secretary in Ford Motor Company. This made possible the theft and later negotiation of large numbers of payroll checks. Following her arrest by the FBI, Ebony again changed occupations. During her sojourn in Detroit, she developed a sexual liason and friendship with an official in the state Department of Motor Vehicles. They made a very simple and mutually profitable arrangement. For $500 cash he would furnish her with a false registration and title for any auto. Ebony would then visit the local new car dealers for a demonstration ride. The auto would be driven to a nearby city and sold. When arrest seemed inevitable, Ebony moved again. In commenting on life, she observed that, "I have dedicated myself to crime."

Pamela, like Ebony, was also an attractive black woman of 24. There any similarity ends. Pamela always had lived in Washington. She had trouble in school and dropped out at 17 after finishing the ninth grade. A year later, her husband offered her the first "fix." Pamela stated that she had never personally committed an illegal act; however, she knew that her husband was deeply involved in forgery and dealing. He supplied her habit for five years while she worked an assortment of jobs, usually as waitress. Pamela had no idea of the cost of the drugs she had been using. For her NTA became the only logical choice following her husband's arrest.

Mike had always been in trouble. Seven years ago at the age of 14, he began shooting heroin. Before that he admits fighting with weapons, shoplifting, gambling, and chronic truancy. He left school at 16. As the habit grew, Mike gave up shoplifting for robbery—his principal source of income supplemented by some dealing. Although he had never served any long sentences, Mike had been arrested seven times. In 1969 he was arrested for and eventually acquitted of robbery and murder. Mike is very street-wise. He does not mind talking about either charge because of "that double jeopardy shit."

Tyrone, now 23, also has used heroin since he was 14. Rather than drop out of school because of drugs, Tyrone has finished a year of college and plans to continue. Unlike most addicts, Tyrone had not been engaged in any delinquent or criminal acts before his drug use. He notes, however, that the older friend—now dead from an overdose—who turned him on was both a burglar and a stick-up man. His friend's "training" enabled him to support a habit that later grew to $60 a day. Although Tyrone admits an extensive pattern of burglary, dealing, robbery, and shoplifting to finance his needs, he claims never to have been arrested for anything.

Occasionally, some of the reported criminal exploits are quite unusual. With a year of college, *Dennis* was better educated than most addicts. He had a polished quiet manner and was obviously very bright. Dennis and his brothers had always been thieves. Before beginning heroin use at 17, Dennis regularly participated in gambling, boosting, joyriding, robbery, and burglary. Four years later Dennis' father stole $210,000 worth of U.S. Treasury checks. With the aid of his two brothers, the foursome set up some dummy corporations and successfully negotiated the checks. For Dennis crime was a family affair.

The single most spectacular theft was reported by *John.* At 47 John was older than most addicts, and had been using heroin intermittently since he was 18. John says of himself,

I was considered a good thief, so I would take a whole truckload instead of a few things. Once in North Carolina, I stole a whole trainload of cigarettes. It was high living for a few months until the F.B.I. came. They gave me five fucking years.

John, along with quite a few of his peers, sharply distinguished between the "regular junkie" who avoids violence and the "stone junkie" who specializes in violent crime. He claims never to have committed a violent crime and says quite simply, "The guns started with the younger generation."

Jim is almost half the age of John. Jim is also a stick-up man. He agrees that younger addicts are more frequently engaged in violent crime, and admits that armed robbery is an almost daily means of support for him. Although Jim has been arrested 11 times, 9 for robbery, he has served only three years in prison.

Quite a few addicts do not become deeply involved in crime and support themselves by a curious mixture of regular work and some gainful crime. *Frank* was such a person. Five years ago at the age of 20, Frank began using heroin while in college. Prior to that he describes himself as both a good student and a good citizen. With the development of a habit costing between $30 and $50 a day, Frank quit school and found a job as a manager in a retail clothes store. He has worked there for four consecutive years. Frank also admits regular dealing and "a few" burglaries. He has three arrests: two for possession of drugs and one for receiving stolen property.

The mixture of jobs and crime during addiction is the modal response to the increased cost of living. Only 29 percent of the sample stated that they never worked while addicted. On the other hand, 58 percent stated that they worked regular part-time or full-time jobs during most of the addicted period. The range of reported jobs includes: janitor, truck driver, secretary, painter, recreation counselor, cashier, dress maker, used car salesman, trash man, electrician, nursing assistant, stock clerk, drummer, carpet layer, cook, construction, auto mechanic, and textile worker. One fellow even claimed to have been a special policeman for several years while he was strung out.

In a few cases the signs of psychopathology were readily apparent. *Malcolm* was a 31-year-old Caucasian who felt compelled constantly to repeat how lonely he was to whomever would listen. He was extremely nervous and would occasionally jump as if unexpectedly stuck with a pin. When he was 15, Malcolm developed a severe cough and was given a prescription cough syrup containing morphine sulfate. That was the beginning. Following recovery, Malcolm used "everything" except amphetamines and marijuana—both of which he "hated." Malcolm claims to have avoided the usual means of obtaining opiates by becoming expert at forging prescriptions and by faking symptoms that normally dictate the administration of an opiate as a pain killer. He was frequently given prescriptions for percodan, dilaudid, or morphine following a rather elaborate deception. Malcolm would go to a medical clinic or a new doctor and complain of recurring kidney stones. When the usual X-rays were ordered he was ready with some masking tape and a few small pebbles which he taped to his side under the gown. Malcolm did admit to the burglary of a pharmacy one night when he was experiencing withdrawal. He was caught and spent a year in an institution for the criminally insane. Malcolm also admits to occasional rages. Once while playing in a band—his means of support—Malcolm turned on an unappreciative bystander and began flailing him with his saxophone.

David was an athletic-looking black fellow of 30. Originally from Philadelphia, he outlined an extensive and violence dotted background of crime prior to using heroin at 23. Unlike Malcolm, David appeared quite normal until I began to question him about his fund-raising activities while addicted. He admitted to some dealing and robbery but suggested that burglary was his principal source of revenue. He continued to note in a very casual manner that "I used to break into people's homes a lot, but every time I went to the bathroom, God told me not to do that. So now I just break into empty buildings."

On one occasion the interviewer became the object of some abuse. *Phyllistine* was a heavy-set black woman about 5'10" tall and with an openly cynical and suspicious nature. Questions were frequently answered by, "What do you want to know that for?" Early in the interview she said, "Some people call me a dyke. Can you handle it, honey?" The inquiry about activities during addiction was answered by, "I made my living by laying on my back so straight-looking things like you could put it in me." Four of Phyllistine's seven arrests were, in fact, for prostitution.

In some ways the older addicts were the most interesting. These people were less concerned about presenting an image to the interviewer and usually talked freely. Unfortunately, there are very few older addicts. *Charles* was born in 1934 and began shooting heroin 15 years later. Heroin was called "glue" in 1949 and a real habit could be supported on 50 cents a day. Two years later Charles dropped out of school and began a long pattern of larceny and irregular work. Typical of the older addict, Charles avoided violence and was generally uninvolved with crime prior to drug use. Eventually, he was to be arrested 12 times, mostly for larceny.

On the first of several occasions that I was to see and talk with *Errin,* he roared up to the clinic entrance on a chromed, modified Harley 1200. As the helmet came off, the receding grey hair and heavily lined face revealed a man approaching 50. Errin agreed to an interview because those things "do good." Six years after dropping out of school, Errin was introduced to heroin by his brother-in-law—a man rather heavily into forgery and larceny. The two of them began working together and over the years, Errin would build an impressive rap sheet of 20 arrests. All of these were related to either larceny or drugs except one "assault with the intent to kill" charge in 1953. Errin denied any violent crime and said the 1953 charge was from a personal thing. For a period of eight years during the middle of his career, Errin gave up heroin after his release from prison. He resumed his formerly irregular work as a used car salesman and reduced his usual frequency of boosting and forgery. The gradual increase in "chipping" toward the end of this period eventually resulted in a new and expensive habit that continued until his 1971 registration with NTA. Although Errin talked rather freely of past crimes, he refused to discuss the present.

At 56, *William* is one of the oldest addicts on the NTA roll. A friend introduced him to heroin during the Depression when 25 cents would buy an addict a two day supply. William considers himself an "ace mechanic" and claims to have supported his habit without crime until after the war. Although never discontinuing his work as a mechanic, William found it necessary to supplement his income by dealing and procuring. Following the war he acquired a group of three to five "real nice" girls to work for him. William was arrested and convicted in 1947 for procuring and carrying a gun ("only to protect my interests"). He was released after two years, but convicted again in 1953 for the sale of heroin and violation of the "White Slave" act. This time it was an additional seven years. William now repairs bicycles in a small shop in northeast Washington.

The addicts seemed aware that they were part of a special subgroup within the black community. Some more than others made it a point to identify with their version of the "super cool" addict image. Dirty work shirts, coveralls, and boots alternated with stacked shoes, velvet "threads" and "tea shades." All seemed to share the special argot and the ubiquitous Kool cigarettes; I have never observed one smoking another brand. The menthol, they report, "gets you off."

This preoccupation with "getting off" usually is connected with the use and abuse of other drugs besides heroin. Although every respondent in the sample was addicted to an opiate, most were confirmed polydrug users. They acknowledged the use of other drugs, particularly cocaine and "Bam"—a powerful street amphetamine. Occasionally, addicts could be seen dealing these substances in front of their own clinics.

3

Research Findings: Descriptive

Questionnaire Results

It is commonly believed that due to the potency of heroin, casual use or "chipping" as it is called is difficult if not impossible to maintain for any length of time. But inferences from medical research do not support this belief. In the first place, there exists a common myth that heroin is "from twenty to twenty-five times stronger than morphine."[1] It is, in fact, only two and one-half times as potent.[2] All of this refers only to the drug in pure form. The substance sold as heroin on the street contains about 5 percent heroin, the remainder being a variable assortment of inert ingredients such as powdered milk, sugar, quinine, etc. Those reporting rapid addiction to this substance also reported very heavy initial use. Some were so enamored by the sensation that they began "getting down" several times a day. If this initial pattern is sustained, it will produce physical dependence in two to four weeks. For most, however, there was a rather extended period of casual use. The mean number of months between first use and addiction was 9.3. With a median of 4.3 the skewness (2.7) of the distribution toward the lower end is apparent. The reported range in number of months was from one to seventy-two (72). These are, of course, addicts in treatment. By definition, they are failures at casual use. They suggest, however, that there is a sizable pool of such users in the inner city.

Another cherished but somewhat discredited myth is that drug-pushing strangers are the first step on the road to ruin. In this sample only two people reported an initial purchase from a stranger; note the distribution indicated in table 3-1. The perhaps surprisingly large "self-obtained" category is due in large part to the relatively simple technology in snorting heroin.

The early use of narcotics was not generally a solitary affair. Several friends "oiling" in a "shooting gallery" was more the rule than the exception. Seventy-seven (77) percent of the addicts reported that their friends were using either the same or more narcotics than they were during the experimentation phase. Only 14 percent claimed to have had friends who were exclusively nonusers.

Table 3-1
Self-reported Source of First Administered Nonmedical Opiate

A friend by himself	31.7%
A friend with other friends	34.7%
A relative (except spouse)	5.0%
A sexual partner	9.9%
Self-obtained	16.8%
A stranger	2.0%

Note: $N = 101$.

This pattern of activity seems consistent with the rapid narrowing of friendship alignments to include very few nonusing peers. Exactly one-third stated that they spent "no time" with "straight" (nonaddict) friends. An additional 42 percent indicated either "less" or "much less" time spent socially with nonaddicts. One addict summed up the feeling by commenting, "Man, they don't even speak the same language."

Respondents were asked to describe the nature of any crime engaged in by the "five (or so) friends you hung around with then." Not quite one-half (48 percent) suggested that their close friends were regularly engaged in a range of crime from relatively minor to quite serious.

These same five friends also carried a disproportionate risk of later becoming addicted themselves. Only 19 percent stated that none of their friends developed a habit while five was the modal category at 29 percent.

Following addiction 48 percent believed that their friends intensified gainful crime. Eleven (11) percent did not see any change, and 5 percent suggested that there was very little crime either before or after. One addict's explanation for the intensification was that "they were 'turnouts'—a friend had to show them the tricks."

The respondents were queried about knowing any *addicts* whose principal means of support was either robbery, burglary, or larceny. For an affirmative reply, they were asked to indicate the average frequency of this activity. Somewhat later in the questionnaire an identical series of questions were asked about any *nonaddicts* they knew. Although fewer nonaddicts were known, a consistent pattern was found in which addicts committed offenses much more frequently than their nonaddicted counterparts. A few comments by the addicts themselves may help to explain the addict-non-addict differences.

The nonaddict steals "whenever a break comes . . . he don't have to hurry."

"Ex-addicts still do what they did, just not as often."

"They (non-addicts) lay back and wait for a good thing."

A very striking and unsolicited difference between the two groups was offered for the offense of robbery and to a lesser extent for burglary. A number of addicts suggested that the nonaddict or ex-addict was much more enterprising in his stick-ups, and that banks and loan companies were standard fare for many. The average junkie, they suggest, is too busy "getting over" with "nickel and dime stuff" to plan such crimes.

More profitable single offenses certainly would account for a portion of the observed differences between the addict and nonaddict frequencies. One of the women interviewed proffered a little irony on this matter. Her younger brother avoided drugs "to stay out of trouble." As a thief, however, "he went from small things to banks. He got 45 years for a bank job in Virginia." She has never been arrested.

Addicts were probed about the degree of specialization present in the addict criminal career. Approximately 30 percent think most addicts stay with one type of offense. Some of the explanations offered for this opinion were:

"When they change, they get busted."

"He don't have time to learn nothing else."

A few seemed to think that an alternate possibility was more likely, viz., that addicts "stay with one thing until it wears out." Or, "start with one thing; go for a while; then move to a new thing." This group believes that at any given time an addict will be specializing in one type of offense, but over time he will be engaged in a broad variety of criminal acts.

Most (63 percent), however, believed that the addict was purely an opportunist. The prevailing sentiment was expressed by a woman who stated simply that "you can't know just one thing because it might fail." One put the matter more bluntly: "A dope fiend is a dope fiend and he gonna get his anyway he can."

The discussion that follows deals with the average retail daily cost of purchasing street opiates. In most cases this was heroin; but a few addicts used illicitly diverted pharmaceuticals, particularly dilaudid, methadone, and "blue" morphine. Since most addicts are polydrug users, those that admitted use of other substances were asked to exclude them from the estimates. Regular cocaine use, for example, would dramatically inflate these averages. The *retail* price was emphasized to insure consistency. This has the unfortunate effect, however, of inflating the real expense incurred by those who were regular dealers. Finally, some of the respondents did not actually bear the cost of their drug expenses. Eighteen (18) percent reported receiving either money or drugs or both from someone else during a substantial portion of the habit. Women accounted for nearly all of this subgroup. The significance of this situation is developed somewhat later during a discussion of alternative responses to addiction.

Respondents were asked about drug expenses at three different phases of their habit: (1) the initial period following experimentation and beginning with daily use, (2) one year after the initial period, and (3) the final year of street opiate use (see table 3-2).

The most dramatic increase in expense occurs during the first year of daily use. Although the rising cost trend continues into the final year, it was not unusual for respondents to estimate a cost during the last time frame that was similar to or lower than the preceding one. If cost is a reflection of tolerance, then tolerance apparently increases at a decreasing rate following an initially rapid rise.

An attempt was made to rank order the sources of money necessary to support these high costs. Respondents were read a list of illegal activities and asked to choose the item that supplied "most" of the money for other addicts that they "knew well." Following a reading of the list, many addicts responded, "yeah," meaning most of the above. A substantial proportion (22.8 percent) would not make the forced choice. This finding does corroborate the earlier discovery that addicts consider themselves unspecialized opportunists in criminal affairs. Most, however, did make a choice with these results. Dealing was tied at 22.8 percent with "most of the above." Robbery, very significantly, was next at 15.8 percent, followed by burglary (8.9 percent), legitimate job (8.6 percent),

Table 3-2
Daily Cost of Opiates at Three Different Periods of Addicts' Career

Daily Cost in Dollars
During the Initial Period ($N = 92$)

Range	1-90	Standard Error	2.0
Mean	19.4	Standard Deviation	19.2
Median	13.5	Skewness	1.5
Mode	20.0	Kurtosis	2.0

Daily Cost in Dollars
One Year After Initial Period ($N = 83$)

Range	1-200	Standard Error	4.9
Mean	58.1	Standard Deviation	45.5
Median	42.1	Skewness	1.2
Mode	30.0	Kurtosis	0.9

Daily Cost in Dollars
During Final Year of Habit ($N = 86$)

Range	8-250	Standard Error	5.4
Mean	77.9	Standard Deviation	50.3
Median	63.5	Skewness	1.1
Mode	50.0	Kurtosis	0.7

Note: Some respondents were unable to make these estimates.

Table 3-3
Criminal Activities Prior to Regular Drug Use

Frequency of Activity	Type of Criminal Activity (%)			
	Truancy	Vandalism	Auto Theft	Gambling
Never	37.6	89.1	78.2	49.5
Occasionally	32.7	9.9	14.9	28.7
Frequently	29.7	1.0	6.9	21.8
	100.0	100.0	100.0	100.0
	Larceny	Weapons Fighting	Burglary	Robbery
Never	73.3	79.2	84.2	79.2
Occasionally	16.8	17.8	12.8	18.8
Frequently	9.9	3.0	3.0	2.0
	100.0	100.0	100.0	100.0

Note: $N = 101$.

Table 3-4
Frequency of Postaddiction Utilization of Income Sources

Frequency of Activity	Type of Criminal Activity (%)		
	Burglary	Dealing	Larceny
Never	63.4	37.6	62.4
Seldom	19.8 ⎫	17.8 ⎫	15.8 ⎫
Frequently	5.9 ⎬ 36.6	12.9 ⎬ 62.4	7.9 ⎬ 37.6
Very Frequently	10.9 ⎭	31.7 ⎭	13.9 ⎭
	Forgery	Robbery	Gambling
Never	75.2	63.4	71.3
Seldom	11.9 ⎫	21.8 ⎫	12.9 ⎫
Frequently	4.0 ⎬ 24.8	7.9 ⎬ 36.6	5.0 ⎬ 28.7
Very frequently	8.9 ⎭	6.9 ⎭	10.9 ⎭
	Spouse-Kin Friends	Legitimate Work	Other Income[a]
Never	21.8	28.7	72.3
Seldom	16.8 ⎫	13.9 ⎫	5.0 ⎫
Frequently	37.6 ⎬ 78.2	14.9 ⎬ 71.3	12.9 ⎬ 27.7
Very frequently	23.8 ⎭	42.6 ⎭	9.9 ⎭

[a]Again, this is usually prostitution, procuring, and short con.
Note: $N = 101$.

"other" (7.9 percent), larceny (6.9 percent), forgery (3.0 percent) gambling (2.0 percent), and spouse-kin (1.0 percent). The category of "other" was mostly prostitution, procuring, and short con.

In response to whether these illicit activities preceded addiction, 38.6 percent replied that they did not know, 35.6 percent said either yes or yes in some cases, and 25.7 percent said no. The responses on this item were very crime specific. Dealing and prostitution were rarely indicated prior to addiction while the opposite was true for robbery and larceny.

Although these findings on preaddictive crime are interesting, they are essentially the impressions of one group about another. The large proportion who did not know is a good indicator of imprecision. To avoid this problem a series of eight specific questions were asked of the respondents concerning their own delinquent (in the broadest sense) and criminal activities *prior* to regular opiate use (see table 3-3). Since these categories are rather specific, it was unusual to find an affirmative reply on more than a few. Only truancy and gambling produced a majority involvement.

Table 3-5
Self-reported Frequency of Pre- and Postaddiction Serious Crime

Offenses		
	None	At Least One
Before addiction	49	52
After addiction	6	95

Note: Serious crimes are burglary, dealing, larceny, forgery, robbery, auto theft, and weapons fighting. $N = 101$.

Nevertheless, roughly one-fifth admitted preaddictive participation in the serious offenses with the exception of burglary (15.9 percent).

A similar but more detailed series of questions was asked about sources of income *following* addiction. Again, keep in mind that it was unusual for a single individual to specify more than three or perhaps four items (see table 3-4).

The use of family and friends was almost universal. Exploitation took a variety of forms, but urgent requests to "borrow" cash were the most frequent. Some confessed to the outright theft of cash or home items having a ready market. As time passed, however, it became increasingly difficult to continue capitalizing on family and friends as an open resource. Since most of the sample worked, ranging from irregular part-time to regular full-time, legitimate jobs provided considerable income to many. Dealing also was common for two reasons. It is a very profitable enterprise if handled correctly, and it insures the addict of a less expensive supply of heroin, usually of a slightly higher quality. Of the more ordinary gainful crimes, larceny, robbery, and burglary predominated.

Table 3-5 suggests the magnitude of the shift in criminal involvement from pre- to postaddiction when only the more serious offenses are considered. The reader may wish to compare this information with table 4-13, where a more detailed analysis of this transition phenomenon is given.

Only 19.8 percent of the sample have successfully avoided arrest on criminal charges (excluding traffic offenses). The remainder, however, amassed a total of 406 giving an average of 4.02 per person for the entire sample. Excluding those without any arrests the mean rises to 5.01 per person. The distribution of these arrests is provided in table 3-6.

Subsumed under "other" are such offenses as: trespassing,

Table 3-6
Frequency of Arrest by Offense Category

	Total No. of Arrests	Relative Frequency (%)
Burglary	0	79.2
Range: 0-4	1-2	18.8
N = 101	>2	2.0
		100.0
Larceny	0	61.4
Range: 0-16	1-2	24.6
N = 101	>2	14.0
		100.0
Rec. Stolen Property	0	94.1
Range: 0-1	1-2	5.9
N = 101	>2	0.0
		100.0
Forgery	0	91.1
Range: 0-6	1-2	7.9
N = 101	>2	1.0
		100.0
Auto theft	0	93.0
Range: 0-9	1-2	5.0
N = 101	>2	2.0
		100.0
Murder or felony assault	0	86.1
Range: 0-2	1-2	13.9
N = 101	>2	0.0
		100.0
Robbery	0	77.2
Range: 0-9	1-2	18.8
N = 101	>2	4.0
		100.0
Drug offenses	0	58.4
Range: 0-7	1-2	31.6
N = 101	>2	10.0
		100.0
Prostitution or procuring	0	90.1
Range: 0-9	1-2	6.9
N = 101	>2	3.0
		100.0

	Total No. of Arrests	Relative Frequency (%)
Other criminal arrests	0	63.4
Range: 0-9	1-2	26.6
N = 101	>2	10.0
		100.0

assaulting a policeman, gambling, conspiracy to bank robbery, vagrancy, rape, disorderly conduct, fraud, carrying a concealed weapon, unlawful entry, Mann Act, false pretenses, carnal knowledge, Federal Firearms Act (machine pistol), and selling untaxed whiskey.

In spite of the curious mixture of work, welfare, and crime, most (68.3 percent) of these addicts found that the habit eventually became "too expensive." In this respect, of course, the sample is highly biased; because of either expense, arrest, or personal reasons, each had sought treatment.

The participants were asked to describe the modal response of addicts generally to rapidly rising drug costs as a result of tolerance and higher prices. The identical question concerning response to rising costs was then asked of those who felt their own habit had become "too expensive" (see table 3-7).

For those whose habit had become too expensive, three and one-half times as many opted for a cure rather than "hustle" for more money. The situation was reversed for the estimates of what "most" addicts do, with two and one-half times as many suggesting that additional "hustle" is the modal response. The accuracy of what "most" addicts do is open to obvious question. Many of the respondents felt compelled to qualify their choice. Some stated that they would not have come to treatment "if the drugs had been o.k." Others implied that it was the combination of poor quality heroin and high prices. A few pointed to the grim conditions on the street: "Addicts are even sticking up their own dealers."

The decision to seek treatment is affected by many factors, one of which is success at crime. Although this success is influenced by a plethora of personal and situational factors, there is one characteristic that all share: chronic use of opiates. It is not unreasonable to expect that either the soporific effects immediately following use or the debilitating effects of withdrawal would impair criminal performance. Respondents were asked first to describe the intoxication levels of most addicts during the commission of an offense, and then, if appropriate, their own condition during a crime (see table 3-8).

Considerable agreement exists that addicts either will not or cannot hustle when they are high. For most it seems to be a matter of choice. One put it this way, "Don't nobody wanna do nothin' to blow a high." The most interesting discrepancy concerns whether the addict does most of his hustling when he is coming down, or feeling "normal" as many say, or when he is becoming sick. This latter condition prevailed for others but not for the sample addicts who seemed quite defensive about acknowledging any lack of self-discipline. Hustling during early withdrawal is probably more common than most admit.

Regardless of the intoxication level, there was a consensus (74.3 percent) that for such crimes as burglary and robbery, addicts do take more chances and are generally less careful than nonaddict thieves. This lack of caution derives from two possible conditions. For the few addicts who prefer to hustle while high, the effect of opiates is to slow reflexes and impair thinking. Although these effects are not denied, they are considered preferable to being "too shakey" to do the job. The more common problem is the addict who has not "scored" and is beginning withdrawal. Time rather than opportunity or risk becomes paramount. "When they sick, they ready!" was a common sentiment.

It was not surprising, therefore, that 58.4 percent believed that chronic heroin use significantly increases one's probability of arrest. Eleven percent, however, thought that arrest was less likely, while 27 percent saw no difference. Those that saw no difference had usually indicated a "normal" intoxication level during their crimes.

Finally, participants were asked to specify any questions they may have minded or found offensive. Only 4 percent did so, listing the items dealing with criminal records and means of support. A similar list was produced by 11 percent of the respondents when asked to specify those questions on which their friends might prevaricate if they were interviewed. Neither of these indicators is considered significant.

Table 3-7
Reported Variations in Response to Escalating Costs ($N = 101$)

	Perceived Response of Others to Escalating Costs (Percent)	Personal Response to Escalating Costs (Percent)
Control the habit	2.0	4.0
Take a cure—includes arrest	26.7	49.4
Hustle for more money	66.3	13.9
Use cheaper drugs	2.0	1.0
NA or DK	3.0	31.7
	100.0	100.0

Table 3-8
Reported Variations in Intoxication Levels During a Crime

	Perceived Intoxication Level of Others During a Crime (Percent)	Self-reported Intoxication Level During a Crime (Percent)
Was high	4.0	5.9
Was coming down	22.8	40.6
Was getting sick	55.4	14.9
Varied	10.9	8.9
NA	6.9	29.7[a]

[a]This large percentage is accounted for by those who claimed to have committed no crimes and by those for whom the question was somewhat inappropriate as in dealing or prostitution.

Note: $N = 101$.

4

**Research Findings:
Analysis and Discussion**

The previous chapter was a descriptive presentation of the research findings generally. Here a more detailed analysis is attempted of each of the six major research questions that were outlined in the introduction to this book and developed more fully there in the section on methodology and design.

Price Increases and Property Crime

The relationship between property crime and drug costs is a principal concern of this study. As previously indicated, it was hypothesized that a sharp increase in drug prices might precipitate a corresponding increase in gainful crime. This hypothesis was tested for the city of Washington in the following manner.

The Bureau of Narcotics and Dangerous Drugs (BNDD—now the Drug Enforcment Administration—DEA) has published quarterly figures on the average national retail price of heroin since 1968. These three-month periods were then interpolated to produce a curve with 55 data points to correspond with the crime totals of interest during this period. The average national retail price of heroin was used for a very pragmatic reason. Only recently have any separate data been available for the city of Washington. However, these data do correspond rather closely to the national average. Also, the DEA indicates that there is no reason to believe that Washington prices differ significantly from those in other major urban areas.

The data on both heroin costs and crime were then plotted on the same axis to provide a visual impression of their relationship over approximately four years. Inspection shows that the relationship between heroin and crime during this period appears to be an *inverse* association. Also it can be seen that there is some positive correlation among the three rates of reported crimes (see figure 4-1).

Three separate correlation coefficients were selected in an attempt to quantify these visual observations. Since all of the data

52

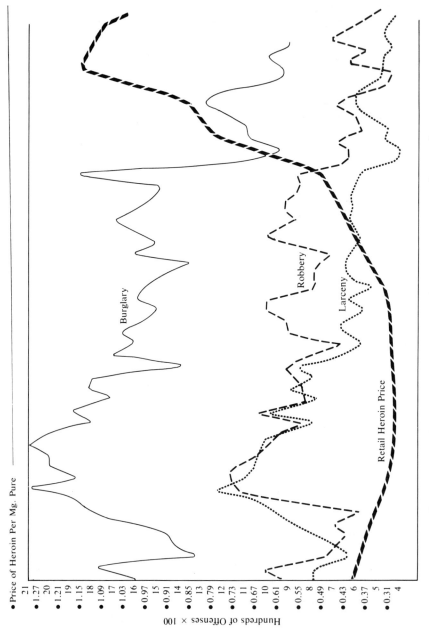

Figure 4-1. Property Crimes and the Retail Cost of Heroin

were interval, Pearson's *r* was an obvious choice. Two non-parametric measures also were felt to have advantages. The significance test for Kendall's and Spearman's coefficients does not require any assumptions about normal distributions. Also, these two coefficients automatically reduce interval data to ordinal. While some information is lost in such a transformation, it has the advantage of reducing the amount of "noise" in weak data.

Table 4-1 is a summary of the quantitative analysis. Two conclusions are readily apparent. Regardless of which coefficient of association is used, all three offense categories are significantly intercorrelated. It seems that the temporal factors influencing the reported rate of one also affect the others in a very similar manner. The second conclusion is that an extremely powerful inverse relationship exists between the retail price of heroin and these offense categories. This relationship does not exist, however, on a micro

Table 4-1
Property Crime Correlated with the Retail Price of Heroin for Washington, D.C.

Matrix for Pearson Coefficients

	Price	Robbery	Burglary	Larceny
Price	——	−0.77	−0.87	−0.65
Robbery	−0.77	——	0.84	0.68
Burglary	−0.87	0.84	——	0.83
Larceny	−0.65	0.68	0.83	——

Matrix for Kendall Coefficients

	Price	Robbery	Burglary	Larceny
Price	——	−0.50	−0.62	−0.54
Robbery	−0.50	——	0.63	0.48
Burglary	−0.62	0.63	——	0.64
Larceny	−0.54	0.48	0.64	——

Matrix for Spearman Coefficients

	Price	Robbery	Burglary	Larceny
Price	——	−0.69	−0.81	−0.74
Robbery	−0.69	——	0.81	0.66
Burglary	−0.81	0.81	——	0.81
Larceny	−0.74	0.66	0.81	——

Note: $p < 0.001$ all coefficients. $N = 55$ months.

level. Month to month fluctuations in the retail price of heroin do not correlate with the changes in reported property crime. The Spearman coefficient for the corresponding changes in the retail price of heroin and reported robbery for all 55 months was only -0.0883. Incremental changes in the cost of heroin had little immediate effect on property crime. The interaction of these two factors is actually rather complex and is discussed in some detail below.

Interpretation

There are two variables here: the retail price of heroin and property crime. It has been shown that sharply increased heroin costs do not produce corresponding increases in property offenses. The remaining question is whether the reverse is true. Do escalating heroin prices act as an independent variable in forcing down property offenses? Or is the observed relationship merely an example of correlation without causality? The following paragraphs explore the possible conditions affecting the variance in each.

The shifts in the price of heroin are, perhaps, the easiest to account for. No significant adjustments have been made in either drug penalties or the likelihood of prosecution during the period in question. In other words, there has been no consistent attempt to increase the "crime tariff" such as occurred in New York with the recently revised drug law. The price of heroin then becomes subject to the basic law of supply and demand, the former being the more critical in this case.

Beginning in 1969 the Bureau of Narcotics and Dangerous Drugs intensified efforts to increase large-scale seizures of narotic drugs, both domestic and foreign. This effort was aided by substantial increases in manpower and money. The success of this campaign is indicated by the BNDD data in table 4-2.

Not unexpectedly there were two effects from these seizures. The price of heroin rose and the quality of the drug declined. Average retail purity levels in Washington during this time period are as follows:

1969	1970	1971	1972
9.1%	7.7%	6.0%	4.5%

Source: DEA, 1974.

Table 4-2
BNDD Opiate Seizures

	Total Domestic Seizures (Lbs.)			
	1969	1970	1971	1972
All opiates	452	721	1,599	1,102
	BNDD Foreign Cooperative Seizures (Lbs.)			
	1969	1970	1971	1972
All opiates	2,691	2,472	4,648	21,899

Source: BNDD 1973.

The shifts in reported property crimes are not so easily accounted for.

The possibility that reported offenses were "adjusted" by the police department for political reasons always should be considered. In this case, however, there is no evidence indicating such an occurrence. There are, in fact, several indicators to the contrary. Auto theft is known to be a crime that is very accurately reported and one for which "adjustments" would be difficult if not impossible to make. The fluctuations in reported auto theft closely correspond to the changes noted for robbery, burglary, and larceny during the period in question. Any significant manipulation of data would have disrupted this correlation.[a] An additional significant factor is that the Statistical Office of the Metropolitan Police Department states that there were no changes in reporting guidelines or procedures between 1968 and 1973. This statement confirms the observations of this writer who was assigned to the Patrol Division for a considerable section of the experimental period. This downward trend in reported offenses for Washington preceded slightly but corresponded to a similar national trend. The 1972 *Uniform Crime Report* indicates that for 58 cities across the country with populations exceeding 250,000, there was a 9 percent decline in Part I offenses [b] between 1971 and 1972. For cities of one million or more the average decline was 12.5 percent. Whatever the factors are that precipitated

[a] The Pearson coefficient between robbery and auto theft, for example, is 0.56, $p<0.01$.

[b] Auto theft, criminal homicide, forcible rape, robbery, aggravated assault, burglary, larceny-theft.

this decline, it would be unreasonable to expect that Washington would be exempt from their influence.

Local factors that could influence the crime rate also were evaluated. A frequently overlooked variable is shifting age composition. During the late 1960s, Washington experienced a steady increase in its population between the ages of 15 and 24. From 111,400 in 1968 this group expanded to 145,250 in 1970, a 30 percent increase in two years. Beginning in 1970, however, the pattern changed to one of more stability. For 1971 and 1972, there was a very slight decline to 144,000 and 143,500 respectively.[1] Both street crime and addiction are clearly age-specific. A rapidly expanding population in the age group most vulnerable to crime will precipitate—other things being equal—a rise in crime. In the same manmer, stabilization of this population normally should produce a corresponding change in street crime. Since reported crime declined rather than stabilized, it is apparent that other factors also were at work. Only a few limited inferences can be made from the demographic changes discused here. Age composition was probably more of a factor in the reported increase in crime than in its decrease. Had the expansion of that group continued, however, it is unlikely that the reported decline in property offenses would have been so significant.

The role of law enforcement during this three-year decline in reported crime is probably significant. Although periodic "crackdowns" on crime are standard fare in most urban departments, few are blessed with the resources to do anything but vocalize. Washington was, however, to become the model crime-free city. By act of Congress, large sums of money were set aside to increase substantially an already large police department. From fiscal year 1968 to fiscal 1971 the actual strength of the department increased from 2,952 to 4,886—a 66 percent increase. Table 4-3 shows these changes including a separate category combining subtotals in patrol, criminal investigation, and tactical force. These three units constitute the effective manpower total directed against crime. The subtotal changes are substantial and amount to a 58 percent increase over the indicated period. Furthermore, these increases do correspond in time with the decline in reported crime. The rapid rise in effective police manpower was almost certainly a factor in the reported decline.

To this point in the evaluation, the rise in the price of heroin and the corresponding fall in crime have been analyzed as functionally

Table 4-3
Washington, D.C. Police Manpower Data

	FY 1968	FY 1969	FY 1970	FY 1971
Patrol, CID, & tactical	1,078	1,171	1,403	1,705
Grand total	2,952	3,535	3,907	4,886

Source: *D.C. Police Annual Reports*, 1968-71.

autonomous events. Large seizures of opiates have forced up prices, while crime has declined as a result of greater law enforcement resources in a more stabilized population. It is likely, however, that in addition to these factors, a functional relationship *does* exist. That relationship involves the advent of methadone in Washington in a deteriorating heroin market.

As noted earlier, the large seizures by the BNDD had two immediate effects. The price of heroin rose while its potency deteriorated. At approximately the same time (early 1970) the Narcotics Treatment Administration (NTA) began accepting addicts into a program of methadone maintenance and/or methadone detoxification. By 1971 NTA was firmly established with more than 2,500 addicts registered in some program. A year later this figure had risen to 3,990. Meanwhile, the number of active (untreated) addicts peaked in Washington in 1971 and has been declining since then. A combination of urine surveys both at D.C. Jail and Superior Court together with the overdose death formula (1 o.d. for every 200 addicts) has produced the estimates shown in table 4-4. Two identical studies at D.C. Jail four years apart corroborate this trend. In 1969 a random selection of 225 offenders entering D.C. Jail were given urine tests and interviewed. It was determined that 45 percent of them were heroin addicts. In 1973 the same procedure was followed for 200 entering offenders. The proportion had dropped to 22 percent.[2]

This decline, although made possible in part by NTA, was ac-

Table 4-4
Estimated Active Addicts in Washington, D.C.

	1970	1971	1972	1973
Active addicts	14,000	17,000	14,000	8,000

Source: NTA Research, 1974.

Table 4-5

Arrest Rates of Narcotics Treatment Administration Addicts Before and After Treatment, 1968-72

	Arrest Rate[a]
2 years before treatment	3.1
1 year before treatment	4.1
1 year after treatment	2.9
2 years after treatment	1.8

includes inactive patients

Note: $N = 423$.

[a]Number of arrests for criminal violations in Washington, D.C. per 100 man-months. See B. Brown and G. Brewster, "A Comparison of Addict Clients Retained and Cost of Treatment," *International Journal of the Addictions* (in press).

celerated by shifts in the economics of heroin, in the criminal opportunity structure, and in the social "acceptability" of heroin use in the ghetto.

Almost all of the addicts interviewed report that "the dope really began getting bad" in 1971 . Many cited the quality of heroin together with its rapidly rising price as the reason for giving it up. Most reported hustling large sums of money for a habit that would no longer get them "high."Methadone maintenance or detoxification through NTA became a logical option for many addicts—perhaps one-third of them.

Although a detailed analysis of effectiveness criteria for the NTA program is not within the purview of this undertaking, several comments are in order.

NTA has no estimates of the number of addicts that detox in one of their facilities and then reappear later with a new heroin habit. There does seem to be an informal consensus, however, that many addicts do use treatment as a means of controlling habit costs and reexperiencing the "high." The impact of treatment on crime for this group is obviously variable. One study did attempt to show the impact of treatment on crime. Arrest rates for 423 addicts were tabulated for two years before and after program entry with the results shown in table 4-5. This modest reduction appears similar to the results generally indicated by the recent literature on methadone.

Interview data provide some insights into the mechanism causing this reduction. Many of the interviewees know nonaddicts or

ex-addicts who are regularly involved with crimes of theft. Tw
fairly consistent observations are made about these offenders. Their
crimes are less frequent than those of the addicts, and a single
"sting" is more likely to involve a larger amount of goods or money.
Addicts say of themselves that they are too busy "getting over" with
smaller, easier jobs to plan anything significant. Because of the
pressure of time and the lack of planning, the addicts almost uniformly believe that they are more likely "to get busted" than a
nonaddict or ex-addict in a similar line of work. Since neither arrest
rates nor reported offenses reflect amounts taken, the decline in
each is probably a result of some ex-addicts giving up theft and
others continuing it on a reduced scale that would resemble more the
pattern of a nonaddict thief.

In addition to law enforcement and economic pressures against
heroin use, there is a new feeling about the drug: heroin is less
"acceptable" than it once was. Although no Harris polls exist on the
subject, the expression "Scag's a drag" is reflective of the change.
Being stoned on junk and hustling like an animal are no longer
"cool." It is inconsistent with the newly emerging black dignity and
self-awareness. Peer pressure now seems to be more against than
toward opiate use.

The following summary seems warranted by the facts. The
powerful association observed between the price of heroin and
gainful crime is somewhat deceptive. Heroin costs and quality are
not the only significant independent variables. Other factors have
been found likely to contribute to the strength of the observed
relationship. The substantial increase of law enforcement resources
in a stabilized population, the arrival of a massive methadone
maintenance-detox program in a deteriorating narcotics market, and
a changing social environment in the city have combined with rising
heroin costs to produce a corresponding decline in property offenses. These relationships are illustrated more clearly in table 4-6.

Price Increases and Personal Response

It was hypothesized rather simply that the sudden increase in drug
prices, which was just detailed, together with the addict's increasing
tolerance for heroin, would be the controlling variables in creating a
personal and economic crisis for the addict. Two principal responses

Table 4-6
Principal Factors Affecting Relationship of Property Crime and Retail Heroin Costs

| | Chronological Sequence | | | | |
	1968	1969	1970	1971	1972
NTA enrollments	No such program		Established spring of this year	2,500	3,990
Total D.C. Police manpower	2,952	3,535	3,907	4,886	4,981
D.C. population, ages 15-24	111,400	128,300	145,250	144,000	143,500
Heroin purity, retail level	Not available	9.1%	7.7%	6.0%	4.5%
Total BNDD opiate seizures in lbs.	Not available	3,143	3,193	6,247	23,001

Source: All data combined from previous tables.

to this crisis were considered likely. The addict could either take a cure or intensify criminal activity. With knowledge of the average costs of the habit at different stages of the drug career, it was expected that cost would have significant predictive value in determining a point or a range in which this crisis was most likely to occur. Finally, for those whose habit had grown "out of hand" (too expensive), which factors were most salient in predicting the response to this crisis?

Not all respondents believed that their habit had, in fact, become "too expensive." Approximately 40 percent entered treatment for other reasons. Also, there was a small group who did not bear the costs of addiction for at least a portion of their habit and for the duration in some cases. This group (18 cases) was considered separately. Given these variations in circumstances, it seemed reasonable to expect certain between-group differences in such matters as opinions and career tracks. Accordingly, table 4-7 displays a comparison among selected items.

The most significant feature in this three-way comparison is the *lack* of any important differences. Only a few things appear worthy of note. As expected, the "too expensive" group averaged a somewhat longer habit (not significant). They were also more likely to believe that other addicts would choose a cure in response to rapidly rising costs. Quite unexpectedly, there appears to be *no*

Table 4-7
Demographic and Attitudinal Comparisons Between Addicts Who Differ in Response to Cost Pressures

| Demographic Factors | Were Habit Costs Perceived as too Expensive? | | | | Respondent Did Not Bear Costs | |
| | Yes (N = 59) | | No (N = 23) | | (N = 18) | |
	Mean	Median	Mean	Median	Mean	Median
Year of birth (19__)	46.1	48.8	45.6	46.1	46.8	48.5
Age at first opiate use	18.7	17.8	19.2	18.6	20.3	19.5
No. of months between first use & addiction	8.8	4.3	10.3	4.0	9.6	5.5
Initial daily cost	19.9	10.8	15.1	13.5	23.9	18.5
Daily cost one year later	58.9	47.9	55.3	42.5	59.5	32.5
Daily cost during final year	77.7	61.9	82.5	66.3	72.0	60.0
Total no. of years of regular use	5.5	4.1	4.9	4.0	3.4	3.0

| Beliefs About Other Addicts' Response to Rising Costs | Were Habit Costs Perceived as too Expensive? (Percent) | | Respondent Did Not Bear Costs (Percent) |
	Yes (N = 59)	No (N = 23)	(N = 18)
Control habit through lower drug intake	3.4	0.0	0.0
Take a cure: Includes incarceration	30.5	17.4	27.8
Hustle for the extra money	59.3	78.3	72.2
Use cheaper drugs	1.7	4.3	0.0
Missing value	5.1	0.0	0.0
	100.0	100.0	100.0

relationship between final costs and the belief about whether a habit has become too expensive. An analysis of variance for costs during the final year for the two groups produced an F ratio of almost zero (0.11). A similar operation was performed comparing initial daily costs and costs one year later against beliefs about whether the habit was too expensive. Again F ratios approached zero. Clearly, daily cost has no predictive value for that question.

If cost is not a critical factor here, perhaps income is. No questions were asked directly relevant to income because of the pretesting discovery of wide fluctuations in response and general inability to answer within any consistent context. Addicts were, however, asked the sources of income (legitimate and otherwise) and the frequency with which they utilized this source. For the nine items listed, each carried a weight of 0 (never) to 3 (very frequently), producing a range for each individual from 0 to 27. An assumption was made that on the average, higher scores would denote greater income. These scores were then correlated with variable 72 (too expensive?) and variable 74 (if too expensive, what was the response?) No association was observed for variable 74, while a weak positive correlation was noted for variable 72 (Spearman's $r = 0.122$, $p < 0.11$). Although insignificant, the correlation would tend to indicate that accelerated acquisitive activities are associated with the belief that the opiate habit has grown too expensive. Given the low level of significance, this finding should be viewed with extreme caution. Furthermore, it is very possible, perhaps likely, that income is not the real independent variable here. The fact of having to engage regularly in a broad range of gainful activity may itself be the source of the belief.

It is reasonably clear at this point that respondents were not making a literal interpretation of the question on habit expense. Cost was evaluated in terms other than money. This is an appealing interpretation if one considers the uniformly large expenditures beyond the first year of the habit. Given a mean final daily cost of $78 for the entire group, and the fact that only 7 percent were paying less than $25 per day, a confined reading of the question would show a habit too expensive for nearly everyone. These high costs, it will be recalled, are not limited to the final year. After only one year, the mean daily expense was in excess of $58. In sum, cost, measured in dollars, is a relatively minor constituent in a complex of factors affecting the more general concept of habit manageability.

In an effort to determine if any particular criminal characteristics had predictive value for the question of habit manageability, several types of analysis were employed. A series of 2×2 tables were generated by cross-tabulating each type of income source (criminal and noncriminal) with variable 72 (too expensive?). Chi squares consistently remained near zero. In no case did significance levels drop below 0.20. Although this procedure is more methodologically conservative, it does not allow for the possibility of a pattern of activity, as opposed to single items, producing a consistent response of either yes or no for variable 72. A multiple regression analysis was, therefore, done using all income sources (variables 41-49) against the dependent variable (72). The cumulative R^2 was 0.078

indicating that the *unexplained* variation in the dependent variable is an extremely high 92 percent. This confirms the previous observation that the choice of income source is quite unrelated to the perception of whether one's habit remains unmanageable.

Unlike the source of income, the degree of involvement in crime is significantly linked with beliefs about habit manageability. The reader may recall that sample respondents were dichotomized into two groups, marginal and confirmed, based on self-reported pre-addictive and postaddictive crime, and on arrests. Note the differences in distributions in table 4-8.

The nearly random distribution in the left portion of the table contrasts with the grouping observed in the right portion. Over three-fourths of the addicts identified as having a confirmed criminal life-style perceived their habits as unmanageable. A similar but insignificant pattern also was observed based upon arrests. Although positing a causal direction is frequently a risky enterprise, analysis to be presented in a later section tends to indicate that addiction in this polity is a self-limiting process. The intensification of crime so necessary to pay the exorbitant costs of addiction later becomes a principal factor in the waning attractiveness of the vice.

Advancing age plays some part in this process, although the realities of its impact have muted its presence. There are few old addicts. Many have died, are in prison, or are unidentifiable by conventional research. Fewer than 10 percent in this sample were over 35. A Pearson correlation of variable 72 (too expensive?) with age during final year of habit (variable 76) was nearly zero (0.10). A breakdown for an analysis of variance revealed that the mean ages for the two groups were only a year apart. The F ratio was, of course,

Table 4-8
Habit Manageability and Self-reported Crime

Too Expensive? (Manageable?)	Self-reported Preaddictive Crime		Self-reported Postaddictive Crime	
	Marginal (N = 70)	Confirmed (N = 29)	Marginal (N = 31)	Confirmed (N =68)
Yes	69%	72%	55%	77%
No	31%	28%	45%	23%
	Corrected chi square = 0.019		Corrected chi square = 3.749	
	Not significant		$p \leq 0.05$	

extremely low. Table 4-9 is illustrative of both the compressed distribution of ages and the close correspondence between observed and expected values.

A variable related to age is "total number of years of habit" (variable 75). This does correlate weakly with variable 72. Those indicating "yes"—the habit was too expensive—had a slightly longer length of habit, 4.8 years compared with 4.0. Unfortunately, no differences were significant. Direct evidence linking age and length of habit to beliefs about manageability is weak indeed. As noted previously, however, this situation is believed to be more an artifact of the sample than a reflection of the situation.

The final portion of this section attempts to explain the variation found in response to the perception of most that the habit had grown unmanageable. As pointed out earlier in table 3-7, only two responses were chosen consistently: take a cure or hustle for more money. In practical terms, a given respondent could have done both several times over a period of years. For those situations they were asked to explain what they did during the first time only. This requirement has the effect of partially minimizing the extreme bias of the sample by moving the time frame for many away from the present. Since without exception, each person interviewed was in treatment, all had ultimately taken a cure.

With that caveat in mind, there are several interesting observations. Given the findings of the previous section, it should not be

Table 4-9
Age During Final Year of Addiction by Belief About Habit Manageability

Habit too Expensive? (Manageable?)	Age Groupings						Total Frequency and Average Proportion
	0-19	20-24	25-29	30-34	35-44	45-55	
Frequency *No*	1	15	6	4	3	0	29
Proportion (%)	6.3	34.9	31.6	40.0	42.9	0.0	29.9
Frequency *Yes*	15	28	13	6	4	3	69
Proportion (%)	93.8	65.1	68.4	60.0	57.1	100.0	70.1
Total	16	43	19	10	7	3	98
Average (%)	16.2	43.4	19.2	10.1	7.1	3.0	100.0

surprising that cost at all stages of the habit had no visible impact on the alternatives chosen by the addicts. The complete lack of apparent relationship is revealed by table 4-10.

Readily accessible nonpunitive treatment has been available in Washington only since 1970 and the coming of NTA. Prior to that many older addicts saw no viable alternative to additional hustling. Age and response are, therefore, strongly related as indicated in table 4-11. By the time a crisis appeared for the younger addicts, cure in the form of methadone maintenance or detoxification became a very acceptable alternative.

Table 4-10
Relationship Between Drug Costs at Different Stages and Response to Perceived Crisis
(Analysis of Variance)

			Needed for $p \leq 0.05$
Average initial daily costs and response	$F = 0.04$	N.S.	2.7
Average costs one year later and response	$F = 0.76$	N.S.	1.9
Average costs during final year and response	$F = 0.10$	N.S.	3.2

Table 4-11
Self-reported Response to Habit Costs by Age During Final Year of Habit

	Age During Final Year of Habit		Total Frequency and
Response to Habit Costs	*Under 26*	*Over 25*	*Average Proportion*
Take a cure:			
(Expected value)	(33)	(17)	
Frequency	37	13	50
Proportion (%)	88.1	59.1	78.1
Hustle more:			
(Expected value)	(9)	(5)	
Frequency	5	9	14
Proportion (%)	11.9	40.9	21.9
Total	42	22	64
Average (%)	65.6	34.4	100.0

Note: Corrected chi square = 5.51. $p \leq 0.02$.

With one curious exception, no other factors were found to be significantly linked to response variation. Although dealers and nondealers were equally likely to believe their habits had grown too expensive (chi square = 0.005), 93 percent of the dealers who decided their habit had become unmanageable chose cure rather than hustle. That breakdown is contained in table 4-12. No other income source produced a similar distribution.

The explanation for this phenomenon is found in the nature of dealing. Many newly addicted persons turn to selling drugs as a convenient form of self-support. It does not require a great amount of skill, and it is usually quite profitable. It is also a "hassle." Street level dealers are caught in the middle. Quite literally, they are cheated by the people who deal to them; they are robbed by their customers; and they are harassed by the police. In spite of all this, some do well enough and never perceive their habits as unmanageable. For those that do, however, hustling more is an untenable alternative. Dealing was chosen as the primary means of support because other alternatives were less desirable due to a lack of skill, mettle, or inclination for other forms of crime. With both first and last resorts considered unacceptable, cure emerges as the favorite choice.

Table 4-12
Utilization of Dealing and Response to Habit Costs

Response to Habit Costs	Narcotics Dealing During Habit		Total Frequency and Average Proportion
	Never	Frequently	
Take a cure:			
(Expected value)	(28)	(22)	
Frequency	24	26	50
Proportion (%)	66.7	92.9	78.1
Hustle more:			
(Expected value)	(8)	(6)	
Frequency	12	2	14
Proportion (%)	33.3	7.1	21.9
Total	36	28	64
Average (%)	56.3	43.8	100.0

Note: Corrected chi square = 4.88. $p \leq 0.05$.

67

Social Policy and Criminal Careers

It has been thoroughly established that criminal income is a necessary supplement if not the entire basis for supporting an opiate habit
in this country. Only 6 percent of this sample denied any gainful
criminal acts during the addicted period, and most of these were
women claiming to have expenses paid by either husbands or
boyfriends. It is not sufficient to note only that 94 percent of the
addicts engaged in some property offenses: one should also ask not
only what proportion would have been similarly occupied if it had
not been for the opiate habit, but also to what extent did a commitment to a criminal life-style appear to be present. Conviction for
a single act of shoplifting and for a daily string of burglaries both
entitle one to be called thief. The practical difference, however, is
quite apparent.

The basic design of this question has been explained previously.
It represents a unique attempt to quantify the *independent* impact of
opiate addiction on criminal careers. The changes observed in this
sample are outlined in table 4-13. The criminal involvement of the
respondent is classified both before and after addiction, the former
based upon self-report and the latter on both self-report and arrest
data. To repeat briefly the basis for classification, *naive* means no
involvement in crime (other than drugs) or no arrests despite involvement. There were a few extreme cases classified as confirmed
under self-report and naive under arrest. The distinction between
confirmed and *marginal* lies in both the seriousness of the offenses
and their pattern over time.

The changes revealed by this table are rather large. Using the two

Table 4-13
**Criminal Life-style Sequences by Pre- and Postaddiction Indexes of
Criminality**

Criminal Career Sequences	Preaddictive Crime by Self-Report	Postaddictive Crime by Self-Report	Crime by Arrest
Confirmed	29	68	50
Marginal	39	27	32
Naive	33	6	19
	72	33	51
	101	101	101

self-report indexes, the increase in the number of confirmed individuals is 134 percent. The somewhat smaller figure (72 percent) obtained by comparing arrest and preaddictive is accounted for by variations in criminal skill and serendipity.

Without control, however, none of the observed differences are more than suggestive of the impact of addiction. As pointed out in the introduction to this book, a nonaddict control will correct this deficiency. A random selection of nonaddict criminal records provides a basis for positing the expected proportions in the cells confirmed and marginal for those criminals not saddled with the burden of a habit. Since arrest data only and identical criteria for dichotomizing are used, the discrepancies between observed and expected values found in table 4-14 may be assumed to be the result of maintaining an opiate habit in our present legal system.

Computation of Yules Q—a relatively direct coefficient of association—gives a rather high -0.63. Chi square $= 12.7$, almost double that needed for an α of 0.01. Only 18 percent (9 of 50) of the nonaddicts have developed a confimred criminal life-style. It has been suggested that the fact of addiction sharply increases the probability of adopting such a life-style. If this probability were not substantially altered, one would expect approximately 18 (18 percent of 101) in the cell postaddiction-confirmed. In fact, the cell contains 50—an increase of 178 percent over expected. This figure may be considered an approximation of the *increase* in persons adopting a confirmed criminal life-style as the result of addiction.

Table 4-14
Criminal Career Differences Between Addicts and Nonaddicts

Sample Source	Marginal (includes Naive)		Confirmed		Row Total
	Expected	Observed	Expected	Observed	
Postaddiction criminals (from this study)	(62)	51	(39)	50	101
Nonaddict criminals (from police records)	(30)	41	(20)	9	50
Column Total		92		59	151

Age, the Year of Addiction, and Crime

This section is a rather straightforward attempt to describe the basic relationship between age, the year of addiction, and crime. It was previously hypothesized that age at addiction onset and criminal activity during addiction should vary inversely due to the younger addicts' increased contact with and dependence upon the criminal subculture. In addition, the year of addiction (age constant) was thought to have similar predictive value in that the present higher drug prices would produce a more extensive or confirmed pattern of crime.

The age at addiction was defined as the age at first use (variable 007) plus one year, since the average period of experimentation was about ten months. The year of addiction then becomes age at addiction plus the year of birth (variable 004). In order to hold age relatively constant, years of addiction are considered only for those who became addicted between the ages of 16 and 20.

As it turns out, the year of addiction correlates *negatively* with both indexes of postaddiction crime. In other words, as the year of addiction recedes, total involvement in crime increases. This relationship is broken down by sex in table 4-15.

There is no element of time in these calculations; therefore, it is not possible to determine if a more intense period of criminal activity is associated with a more recent year of addiction. However, if one

Table 4-15
Correlations Between the Year of Addiction and Dichotomous Indexes of Criminality
(Marginal and Confirmed)

	Pearson Coefficients		
	Both Sexes (N = 59)	Male (N = 41)	Female (N = 18)
Preaddictive self-report crime	0.083	0.179	0.203
Postaddictive self-report crime	−0.231 $p < 0.05$	−0.169	−0.384 $p < 0.05$
Postaddictive crime by arrest	−0.227 $p < 0.05$	−0.202	−0.306

considers that the preaddictive crime period is relatively fixed, say five to seven years, then the consistent but very weak positive correlations may be indicative of a trend in which similarly aged persons are increasingly likely to be criminally involved as the years grow more recent.

What does appear to be certain is that the significant inverse correlations observed show that addicts faced with a longer period of addiction have both the need and opportunity to amass an impressive catalog of offenses. A similar but more direct interpretation is that a "confirmed" as opposed to "marginal" life-style is increasingly likely to have developed as the year of addiction decreases.

In order to verify this finding, two different but related variables were compared. Total number of arrests was used in place of the postaddictive dichotomies of marginal and confirmed, and total number of years addicted (variable 75) was used in place of the year of addiction. The resulting Pearson coefficient (0.212, $p < 0.02$) clearly confirms that total volume of crime as indicated by arrests is a function of habit length and, therefore, the related year of addiction. It is a matter for future research, however, to prove conclusively whether this volume is more concentrated in recent years.

The impact of the age of addiction upon the addicts' criminal career is unmistakable. As previously hypothesized, younger addicts are much more likely to have adopted a confirmed criminal life-style than their older peers. The observed relationships are outlined in table 4-16, broken down by sex. Again, the sex of the respondent appears to make little difference.

Table 4-16
Correlations Between the Age of Addiction and Dichotomous Indexes of Criminality
(Marginal and Confirmed)

	Pearson Coefficients		
	Both Sexes (N = 101)	Male (N = 71)	Female (N = 30)
Preaddictive self-report crime	−0.220	−0.160	−0.359
	$p < 0.01$		$p < 0.05$
Postaddictive self-report crime	−0.293	−0.223	−0.381
	$p < 0.001$	$p < 0.05$	$p < 0.02$
Postaddictive self-report crime by arrest	−0.145	−0.137	−0.126

As the age of addiction falls, there appears to be an increasing merger of criminal and addict subcultures. Conversely the older initiate has had a longer period of conventional socialization and participates in crime only as necessary.

The significant inverse association between preaddictive self-report and age of addiction points to a very interesting self-selection process. Youth and intensified criminal activity combine to produce a group very vulnerable to both addiction and a continuing pattern of serious crime. This intensified pattern of crime usually peaks several years after addiction or just prior to treatment.

Crime and Delinquency Prior to Opiate Use

Given the social policy significance of preaddictive crime, the dearth of factual material in the literature is rather surprising. As pointed out in the introduction to this book, any generalizations about the criminal life-style of the present day addict are quite invalid without some determination of the nature and frequency of preaddictive crime and the independent impact of addiction on that crime. These and related considerations are developed below.

As Edwin Sutherland so adequately pointed out, crime is an activity learned from one's friends (see table 4-17). It, therefore, is an appropriate starting point to outline this activity. Nearly one-half of these future addicts had friends who were regularly engaged in a variety of criminal acts at an early age. Not surprisingly, many respondents were similarly occupied.

Together the 101 participants accumulated 40 criminal arrests prior to their careers as addicts. The breakdown is given in table 4-18. With one exception, a rather similar pattern exists based on preaddictive self-report data (see table 4-19).

Burglary may be slightly overrepresented in terms of arrests

Table 4-17
Criminal Activity of Closest Friends Prior to Respondent's Addiction

Serious crime (robbery, burglary, etc.)	17.2%
Less serious crime (shoplifting, joyriding, etc.)	30.3%
Little if any crime (some truancy or gambling)	45.5%
Did not have many close friends	7.1%

Note: $N = 101$.

Table 4-18
Arrests of Sample Respondents by Offense Prior to Addiction

Larceny	7
Burglary	6
Robbery	5
Auto theft	5
Murder or felony assault	3
Drug related (any type)	3
Forgery	1
Prostitution	1
Other	9
Total	40

Table 4-19
Delinquent and Criminal Activities Prior to Addiction

	Claimed to be Engaged in Crime (%)		
	Never	*Occasionally*	*Frequently*
Truancy	37.6	32.7	29.7
Gambling	49.5	28.7	21.8
Larceny	73.3	16.8	9.9
Auto theft	78.2	14.9	6.9
Robbery	79.2	18.8	2.0
Weapons fighting	79.2	17.8	3.0
Burglary	84.2	12.9	3.0
Vandalism	89.1	9.9	1.0

Note: $N = 101$.

since some modicum of skill is normally required to insure success. Purse snatching or yoke robbery, on the other hand, requires little more than a strong arm and a swift foot.

To this point the material presented gives a firm impression of early criminal participation by many but not all of the respondents. Using the previously developed criteria to categorize involvement, table 4-20 describes quantitatively the practical shifts along the continuum from thoroughly conventional to thoroughly criminal.

There are several important observations to be made here. For approximately one-third of the addicts there was, in fact, no prior criminal activity. Only a handful maintained such a conventional status following the onset of regular opiate use. The change in marginal status is not so impressive since it both gained from naive

Table 4-20
Criminal Career Changes: Pre- and Postaddiction

Criminal Career Sequences	Preaddiction Self-report	Postaddiction Self-report	Percentage Change
Naive	33	6	−82
Marginal	39	27	−31
Confirmed	29	68	+134
	101	101	

and lost to confirmed. This latter category expanded following addiction from under one-third to over two-thirds of the sample to become the modal form of adjustment.

Together with the analysis performed in the section "Social Policy and Criminal Careers," the independent impact of addiction in this culture on criminal life-styles is quite clear. The mechanism, however, is more open to interpretation. No doubt the need for substantial amounts of cash not available through conventional resources is a principal causal factor in the observed shifts. It is also very likely that powerful social pressures make it very difficult for the fledgling addict to maintain for long any air of pristine virtue. The forced interdependence of the addicts because of the need to share information on police activities, and on sources of money and drugs, would make nonconformance difficult to sustain. Reevaluated in this manner, the causal mechanism involved in producing these shifts is both complex and compelling.

In analyzing the general significance of preaddictive crime, a very natural question becomes: To what extent does the type of offense most commonly committed before addiction have predictive value in pointing to the type of illicit support most likely to develop after addiction?

To answer this, a series of pre-post comparisons was done based upon the respondents' actual experiences. Two issues are important here. Is the presence of an offense prior to addiction a good predictor of its later appearance? Conversely, does its absence before addiction mean that it is unlikely to emerge later? Tables 4-21 through 4-24 show the relationships for the most common offense categories on which comparable data exist.

The importance of the early criminal pattern has been demon-

Table 4-21
Pre- and Postaddiction Presence of Robbery

| | Preaddiction Robbery | | |
	No	Yes	Row Total
No: Frequency	61	3	64
(Expected value)	(51)	(13)	
Postaddiction Robbery			
Yes: Frequency	19	18	37
(Expected value)	(29)	(8)	
Column total	80	21	101

Note: Corrected chi square = 24.91 with one degree of freedom. $p \leq 0.001$. PHI = 0.50.

Table 4-22
Pre- and Postaddiction Presence of Gambling

| | Preaddiction Gambling | | |
	No	Yes	Row Total
No: Frequency	45	27	72
(Expected value)	(36)	(36)	
Postaddiction gambling			
Yes: Frequency	5	24	29
(Expected value)	(14)	(15)	
Column Total	50	51	101

Note: Corrected chi square = 15.18 with one degree of freedom. $p \leq 0.001$. PHI = 0.39.

strated beyond doubt. Note that in the case of robbery, its early presence almost insures its continuation after addiction. Only three people acknowledged such an offense before but not after. Likewise, the frequency for those resorting to robbery for the first time after addiction was much lower than expected. Similar observations may be made about the other offenses.

In sum, criminal behavior prior to addiction, frequently a group phenomenon, was indulged in by approximately two-thirds of the respondents with varying degrees of assiduity. Following addiction, those who had not developed any criminal skills either began such

Table 4-23
Pre- and Postaddiction Presence of Burglary

| | Preaddiction Burglary | | |
	No	Yes	Row Total
No: Frequency	60	4	64
(Expected value)	(54)	(10)	
Postaddiction burglary			
Yes: Frequency	25	12	37
(Expected value)	(31)	(6)	
Column Total	85	16	101

Note: Corrected chi square = 10.17 with one degree of freedom. $p \leq 0.001$. PHI = 0.32.

activities as dealing or prostitution, or they were "turned out" (i.e., taught) by their addicted friends. Economic and social pressures make such offers very difficult to refuse. For the remainder of the group their criminal careers following addiction may be viewed as an amplification of a previously established pattern.

Addict and Nonaddict Crime

The intent of this section is to explore tentatively some of the characteristics that distinguish addict and nonaddict crime. Ideally, matched samples of addict and nonaddict burglars, pickpockets, etc. would be questioned similarly. Since this was not possible, the more subjective and anecdotal observations of the addicts themselves must suffice.

As they became relevant, portions of these observations were included earlier; for instance, respondents listed dealing, robbery, and burglary as the three principal sources of revenue for addicts generally (page 42). Addicts are widely and correctly assumed to be responsible for much of the street-level dealing in the inner city. At the level of the small-time pusher and bag man, it is rarely a nonaddict offense. Robbery is more open to dispute. The recent New York study found that "crimes of violence (such as mugging and armed robbery) were infrequently resorted to . . . [and that they] were the least likely type of crime to be committed."[3] This stands in sharp contrast to the situation in Washington. In terms of gainful crime,

Table 4-24
Pre- and Postaddiction Presence of Larceny

| | Preaddiction Larceny | | |
	No	Yes	Row Total
No: Frequency	52	11	63
(Expected value)	(46)	(17)	
Postaddiction Larceny			
Yes: Frequency	22	16	38
(Expected value)	(28)	(10)	
Column total	74	27	101

Note: Corrected chi square = 6.15 with one degree of freedom. $p \leq 0.01$. PHI = 0.25.

robbery is second only to larceny in total number of arrests in this study. It was also frequently cited as a regular pre- and postaddiction activity. There is no ready explanation for the proclivity of Washington addicts to commit robbery. It is possible that the known increase in alcohol consumption may have some violent criminogenic impact, but without confirmation by separate research, this is speculation only.

Robbery is interesting for another reason. It was the most frequently cited example to illustrate some of the typical addict-nonaddict differences. Addiction does, in fact, seem to impose certain constraints upon both the criminal opportunity structure and the frequency of criminal activity. A rather wide consensus exists among respondents that addicted stick-up men engage in robbery more frequently and for smaller amounts than their nonaddict peers. Of those having personal knowledge of addicts engaged in robbery, 74 percent reported the frequency as either daily or two to four times a week. An identical question concerning nonaddicts produced only 20 percent in this combined category. The remainder was either once a week or one to two times a month. A similar comparison for burglary would not be meaningful since 79 percent did not know any nonaddict burglars.

Addicts complained that the recurring need for drug money not only prevented them from "getting over big," but also increased the risks. Some admitted to acts of robbery or theft under circumstances they would ordinarily shun. It is not that the element of risk was not acknowledged by these people; it is that fear of withdrawal seems to produce a panic quite disproportionate to the physiological condition.

Sixty percent of the respondents believed that the arrest of an addict thief was more likely, primarily due to his inability to "lay back" and wait for low-risk "scores." Few seemed to believe that the effect of the drug itself altered arrest probability in any significant manner. The reason for this lies in both the purity of the drug and its pattern of use. Since the quality of heroin began to deteriorate in 1970, addicts say that it takes $100 "to nod." Since the mean daily cost during the final year of the habit was $78, and since addicts usually "oil" at least three times a day, the $25 or so spent on each fix does little more than return the addict to "normal." The majority of respondents (58 percent) would wait until any "buzz" had subsided until they began again the cycle of stealing and oiling.

5

Summary and Conclusions

The focus of this book has been the relationship of addiction and crime as shaped by a social and legal response inimical to the nonmedical use of opiates. The nature of this response has done little to reduce abusive consumption. It has, however, changed the profile and life-style of the opiate addict. To be a "successful" addict in this culture generally requires youth, an urban environment, and a disposition untroubled by the distinction between conventional and criminal. There is, in other words, a self-selection process that precedes the modal and alternative career tracks followed by the opiate addict. This chapter highlights a few of the more significant developmental patterns and influences that characterize these tracks. It concludes by examining some of the implications of this research.

The nonrandom sample used for this research is composed entirely of addicts in treatment. Although considerable care was taken in chapter 3 to compare the characteristics of this sample with those of other known addicts, caution is urged when making generalizations to addicts not identified by any official agencies or to those identified but not necessarily living under similar social and economic conditions.

An analysis of the personal and demographic characteristics of this sample indicates that Washington's future addicts seem little different from their peers. They are black, in their mid-teens, and just beginning high school. Gambling, shooting pool, smoking marijuana, and drinking are recreational activities common to these inner city students. In addition to such innocuous pastimes, most of the preaddicts have committed at least one type of property offense, usually shoplifting or burglary. Increasing truancy usually coincides with these offenses since the ideal combination of empty homes and full stores prevails during normal school hours. A substantial minority also has supplemented their income with robbery.

This information alone indicates that there is no single preaddictive type. The future addict is found all along the continuum from the highly conventional to the confirmed criminal, although there is clear evidence that he is drawn disproportionately from the ranks of the delinquent.

Without the advent of heroin, most with conventional orientations probably would have remained uninvolved in crime. Many of those not heavily involved would have drifted out of crime with advancing age.

Heroin changes all that. For such a diverse group, its appeal seems strongest between ages 18 and 19. Initially it is seen as a new and promising form of unconventional excitement. Later, the recurring need and expense will give it a central place in the addict's life. By now, most have left school. About one-half of those remaining will leave shortly thereafter.

The period of early use is often called the honeymoon. Approximately one-half will develop physical dependence within five months. During this period, drugs are cheap and the "highs" are good. A few "buck-action caps" every week present no unusual financial drain. While all may seem normal, an important change occurs during the honeymoon that will affect the future addict's later life.

A persistent trend has begun that will narrow his friendships to include very few nonaddicts. The significance of this is quite simply that these people are for the most part regularly involved in gainful crime to support an already developed habit. The initiate must now either cease experimentation or be willing to accept new ways. There is no viable alternative and many do, in fact, quit entirely or limit themselves to infrequent use. The others, of course, are the subject of this study.

In addition to developing some descriptive information about the life-style of the individual addict and the influences that shape it, considerable time was spent scrutinizing more macroscopic aspects of the relationship between opiate addiction and crime.

In a quite unexpected discovery, for example, it was learned that over a period of four and one-half years a very powerful inverse association existed between the retail price of heroin and the reported rate of property offense. This finding casts serious doubt on any notion that rapidly rising drug costs might precipitate a corresponding rise in gainful crime as the means of paying additional expenses. The suggested explanation for this phenomenon is rather complex in that several factors were found to be operating simultaneously. Large foreign and domestic seizures of opiates had driven the price of heroin up and its quality down. Within the same period, the purity of street heroin declined by approximately 50 percent. Meanwhile, large increases in law enforcement resources together with a massive scale methadone maintenance-detox program began to affect the crime rate.

Although the precise juxtaposition of these factors is unique to the city of Washington, it seems reasonable to expect that the combination of a deteriorating heroin market and the availability of drug maintenance facilities may have produced similar declines elsewhere. An interesting topic for future research is whether opiate purity levels on the street constitute one of the most important factors in the success of treatment, and indirectly, in the reduction of crime. Using a large number of cities, perhaps a gradient of purity levels could be established that would have predictable conse-quences for both treatment and crime. Within this book, there is some anecdotal evidence for that possibility. The quality of heroin was constantly cited as an important factor in seeking treatment. What seemed to be intolerable was not that so much money was being spent, but that it was no longer buying ''the high.'' A few even suggested that if high quality heroin were available, they would return to it.

A related finding was that the variability in monetary cost had no impact on whether the addict perceived this habit as ''too expen-sive'' (unmanageable). The significant factor in clarifying this perception was whether the addict had a ''marginal'' or ''con-firmed'' criminal life-style based upon self-report data. Three-fourths of those found to be confirmed also believed that their habit had become unmanageable. It appears that benefits are measured in terms of the potency of the narcotic effect and costs are measured in terms of the quality and quantity of trouble necessary to achieve these effects regularly. The addicts' analysis of these costs and benefits includes the amount of cash for the transaction as only an incidental matter.

Economic and social policy concerns do shade into one another. It seemed reasonable to expect that a recurring need to purchase a substance made expensive by a crime tariff would have a strong criminogenic influence on many of the new addicts. For perhaps one-fourth of the neophytes, the intensification of gainful crime is quite minimal. The previously extant pattern of acquisitive behavior was generally adequate to meet the new expense. A second and slightly larger group was compelled to develop and intensify a formerly irregular and unadroit pattern of crime. In both cases, the types of offense engaged in prior to addiction were generally found subsequently. In the case of robbery, this before-after sequence is especially strong. The addicts simply gravitate to what they know best. For approximately one-third, however, there is no earlier pattern to develop. The mandatory life-style changes for these people are dramatic. Some are openly taught how to steal by friends. Others, however, take up relatively unskilled occupations such as dealing and prostitution. These activities, in spite of the fact that they are profitable, are rarely encountered before addiction.

The intensification of crime following addiction is well known. A unique attempt, however, was made in this research effort to demonstrate and quantify the independent impact of addiction on criminal careers. With the use of a demographically similar nonaddict control group, this impact was measured and found to be highly significant. The proportion of addicts who graduate from a marginal to a confirmed criminal life-style was unusually high. This would seem to be documentation of a paradox in social control: The attempt to suppress one type of deviance produces another.

A necessary by-product of this paradox is the merger of the criminal and addict subcultures. To purchase heroin (or any street opiate for that matter) in the amounts required to satisfy a habit is an expensive undertaking. Regular crime becomes the only practical solution. There are other than economic pressures on the new addict to associate with the established group. With the experimentation phase over, knowledge of who has drugs for sale suddenly becomes critical. Fear of withdrawal seems to assume primary drive status. Knowledge of police activities and drug price and purity variations also become both important and unavailable outside the addict-criminal group. The initiate has little choice but to enter the established and informal network—a network held together by nicknames and common needs.

Finally, it was discovered also that the younger an addict is upon entering this network, the more deeply committed he becomes to a confirmed criminal life-style. The shorter period of conventional socialization leaves few alternatives but to pursue what is known best.

All things repeated frequently enough tend to become routine.

The cycle of theft and drug use is no different. After only a few years, the addict begins to be aware of additional changes. The intensificiation of crime initially so necessary to support the habit becomes an important consideration in the decision to terminate it. In addition to the normal tolerance developed by the body, most of these respondents were faced with a combination of rapidly rising drug costs, increased police presence, and declining drug purity. The daily or almost daily hustling for money was no longer providing any real benefits. Its debits, on the other hand, are readily apparent. Over 80 percent were arrested by the police, most several times. Jail or prison sentences were common. Hepatitis, septicemia, skin abscesses, and other secondary pathologies were also common. Social isolation as it both lengthens and intensifies becomes even more difficult to tolerate. In short, addiction in this culture is clearly a self-limiting process. Habits for this sample averaged only four to five years. (Older addicts, not faced with all of the circumstances described above, averaged a slightly longer period of use.)

As suggested earlier the decision to criminalize nonmedical opiate use does not eliminate that use as much as it dictates how that person will live. The harried life of the addict is a product of that decision. To the extent that such an unpleasant existence shortens the period of addiction, the policy of criminalization may be narrowly interpreted as being partially successful. Some of the social costs of this policy, however, should be pointed out.

One of the most distorted views of the relationship between addiction and crime is found in the justification for the widespread and poorly restricted use of civil incarceration. The latent if not manifest function of this operation is to clear the streets of addicts and thereby reduce crime. The state then uses a situation it has created (addict criminality) as the justification for incarcerating the victims of social policy. This is not intended as an apology for addict crime. It is intended to point out that lack of clarity in social objectives has created an absurd situation. If justice is not to be mocked, either repression of this type of deviance or repression of property offenses should be given priority. This study is in firm agreement with the prevailing opinion that addicts are, in fact, responsible for a disproportionate amount of such crime. However, the importance of social policy in generating this condition has not been sufficiently developed or documented in the past.

The effective removal of one-half million people from the social and economic mainstream is certainly an additional cost. In an era when communication with and participation of disadvantaged groups is viewed as critical in developing a more homogeneous and less discordant social order, to not only encourage but make essential the maintenance of such an isolated group seems without justification. The economic and social pressures on the addict to participate in a highly antisocial subculture were noted previously. No such subculture existed prior to the criminalization of nonmedical use, and none is likely to develop without those pressures.

A related third area of concern arises from the fact that the criminalization of the addict produced by the criminalization of nonmedical use is only partially reversible. As this research has demonstrated, the normal socialization of these people is effectively terminated with the onset of addiction. The period of life between 19 and 25 that is normally filled with education and work is now occupied by honing criminal skills. The modest impact of treatment (regardless of type) in reversing this behavior should not be surprising. It is not simply that the addict steals to support a habit; he steals because he has become a thief.

The usual calculus of cost to society for all of this is measured in terms of property stolen. Since addicts are considered essentially passive and nonviolent, it is disturbing to find that there now appears to be a consensus among Washington addicts that violent crime—particularly robbery—is becoming increasingly acceptable among the young. The recently concluded Hayim study (Final Report) also is noted that the incidence of violent crime among addicts appears to be rising. This trend finds support from nationwide data compiled over a ten-year period ending in 1971, which shows that robbery arrests for persons under 18 years of age have increased 234 percent. By comparison, the increase for persons aged 18 and over was only 113 percent.[1]

Given the opportunistic nature of addicts and the fact that cash does not need to be fenced, it seems reasonable to expect that in the future robbery will become more common as a means of support. The inhibitions that restrained the older addict no longer appear to be operative.

This possibility again brings into focus the matter or the intent of our criminal policies. To think of the volume of nonviolent property offenses committed by addicts is unsettling enough without the prospect of a substantial rise in robbery. If the reduction of gainful crime rather than the suppression of deviance is the primary concern, then radical reevaluation of our social control efforts in this field is both necessary and reasonable. The decriminalization of opiate drugs has become an unthinkable alternative only because of the problems produced by its criminalization. Only within this century has its use been so energetically curtailed, and only within this century has its connection with crime been so firmly established.

Policy Alternatives

Few alternatives to our present mode of controlling opiates have been advocated seriously. One of the principal justifications for establishing the prestigious National Commission on Marihuana and Drug Abuse was to make recommendations and suggest alternatives where appropriate. Although the commission acknowledged the complexity of control in this area, and the fact that "the drug problem is . . . part of, rather than the cause of, other social and economic conditions,"[2] the final recommendation by the commission on opiates is really more of the same:

Its [heroin] social cost is considered out of proportion to the number of its users. This reason, coupled with strong symbolism attaching to the use of this drug within affected communities, justifies the highest possible restrictions on availability. . . . The best hope for reducing the social costs of heroin dependence lies in the prevention and treatment areas.[3]

Shortly after the release of the commission's findings and recommendations (1973), the Nixon Administration began to issue statements with supporting evidence that the "war on heroin" had been won. Obviously, if this were true, then the policy of "more of the same" would be justifiable at least. Unfortunately, there is a growing consensus that whatever downtrend in opiate abuse may have occurred in the early seventies is now being reversed.[4] In a special study commissioned by the Drug Abuse Council, the geographical extent and permanence of the downtrend were examined carefully.[5] It suggests that opiate abuse is essentially a cyclical phenomenon with wide fluctuations. The report specifically refers to Washington, D.C. and suggests that the downturn there in heroin use was a local phenomenon made possible by declining drug purity and the fact that "the police were cracking down heavily on distribution, [while] treatment facilities were springing up"—a conclusion closely paralleling a finding of this research.

More importantly, the report demonstrates that long-term solutions to the problem of controlling opiate abuse are yet to be found. While we tinker with the machinery of control, the dual problems of reducing consumption and its attendant social costs remain unabated. The solution of "more of the same" is no solution at all.

The formal labeling and law enforcement activities aimed at a long-term reduction of consumption clearly have been ineffective. Worse, these activities have produced an identifiable subculture— alienated from the general population, with strongly deviant values of its own, and heavily dependent upon gainful crime. By defining the nonmedical use of opiates as evil, and by removing such users from the social and economic mainstream, we have created a worse problem than that for which the cure was intended. This phenomenon is not restricted to drug abuse control as indicated by the more general model stated below.

If the definitions of deviance lead to the removal from the experience of "normal" people of certain deviant persons, the future definitions of deviance will not include the experience relating to those so removed. Moreover, if the action against deviants is such that they are not retained within the general system of values and controls, the new group created by the definition, as well as the residual group, will tend to construct new values and controls. Not only will the parent population cease to include within its experience the information relevant to the deviant, but the deviants may cease to have information regarding normal behavior.[6]

What then is to be done? Chapter 1 discussed some historical and cross-cultural literature that indicated other alternatives to limiting opiate abuse exist, which do not have the unintended consequence noted here of amplifying related forms of deviance. Of particular interest is the approach in the United Kingdom. The British approach is more than the fact that notified addicts may obtain free narcotics; it is "a set" of attitudes toward the entire problem. This rather "matter of fact" set of attitudes seems to be shared by all involved, viz., the police, the addicts, and public officials. The calmer atmosphere is certainly less conducive to the alienation of the opiate user "from the general system of values and controls."

An extended analysis of the British approach would be inappropriate here. However, two aspects of that approach deserve special note as they pertain to the more general discussion of social policy and deviance amplification. The quantity of narcotics being prescribed for each addict is being reduced gradually in a not so subtle attempt to promote abstinence.[7] This move is being resisted by supplemental purchases of "Chinese" heroin and by the use of other soporific drugs, particularly the barbiturates. The second aspect that is somewhat troubling is the fact that British addicts continue to be arrested and convicted for drug-related offenses. A recent British Home Office study reports that two-thirds of the females and 80 percent of the males on the addict registry were *convicted* of drug-related offenses during a two-year follow-up period.[8] The first problem seems to have arisen from conflicting priorities, and if not checked, will compromise seriously the effectiveness of the current approach. The second matter of arrests is also important. While the British addict is arrested more frequently than his American counterpart for drug rather than property offenses,[9] the fact remains that arrest and conviction for a drug offense is a clear indication that the British addict is considered a deviant and a criminal. It can be safely assumed that this perception is not lost on those subject to its stigma. In some sense then, the British and American approaches differ only by degree. From this writer's view, it is an important degree. Nevertheless, the logical question remains, whether even this more limited but formal labeling may be counterproductive and unnecessary.

Perhaps other alternatives should be considered for easing the dual problems of reducing consumption and its attendant social costs.

In 1972 the Vera Foundation suggested a pilot project of heroin maintenance for a small number of addicts who had dropped out of methadone programs in New York City.[10] The plan, which was never realized, was similar to the approach in the United Kingdom only in that known addicts would be given doses of injectible heroin prescribed by clinic physicians. Generally, however, the Vera proposal would have been more restrictive than the policy of the United Kingdom. For example, uncooperative addicts could be terminated from the program and no one would be allowed to remove heroin from the treatment center. Furthermore, addicts would continue to be arrested for the possession and distribution of heroin and other drugs once they left the facility. Given these facts, the Vera proposal would seem to hold few advantages over present policy—not to mention the administrative nightmare of expanding the services of these tightly controlled clinics to meet the needs of approximately one-half million addicts.

If addicts were to have inexpensive and unfettered access to high quality opiates at the times and in the amounts that they may choose, the necessity for a supportive subculture would vanish gradually. There would be no need to provide its members with information on things such as: Who is selling what? How much? How good is it? Where are the cops most-least active? Under present conditions, once the experimentation phase is over, the information on crime and drugs, obtainable only through active participation in this informal network, becomes critical to the new addict. Practically speaking, the choice of maintaining a heroin habit in our present legal system is an almost certain predictor of membership in a subculture whose values and expectations are seriously deviant. It cannot be emphasized too strongly that this condition is an artifact of social policy, and not of the chemical composition of heroin.

Under these conditions the model of deviance amplification noted earlier clearly appears to be operative. To break up the pattern of deviance amplification and free the opiate abuser from dependence on a criminal subculture, one alternative would be to make pure heroin available for inexpensive purchase by anyone aged 18 and over. Under these conditions, a habit could be maintained indefinitely for less than the present cost of smoking cigarettes. Heroin would be an item that could be asked for at most pharmacies. Any promotion of it would be prohibited. Its price would be fixed. All containers would be clearly labeled as to contents and recommended dosage. Prominent warnings also would be included on the toxic and addictive potential of heroin.

While many other opiates are abused, none has the reinforcement potential of heroin, and none under this system could be purchased less expensively. Illicit trafficking in opiates would come to an abrupt halt.

Markets for other illicit drugs probably would be disrupted as many users of an indiscriminate mixture of opiates, cocaine, and barbiturates began to purchase more of the inexpensive and high quality heroin. Nevertheless, if after a sufficient trial period, it became apparent that a seriously deviant subculture was being formed around a sustained black market for another substance, it too could be made available in a similar fashion.

Simple decriminalization is not enough. If possession and use are permitted but sale is not, the continuation of an expensive black market in opiates is assured, and, if that is true, the too familiar association of opiates with gainful crime will continue.

The most obvious problem with this alternative is yet to be addressed. Does this now mean that we will be inundated by a new wave of heroin-dependent persons? Since one avowed purpose of exploring alternatives is to reduce drug consumption, how can legal, inexpensive, and unlimited distribution of heroin be consistent with that end?

It is probable that the number of persons dependent on heroin would begin a gradual decline. The mean age of addiction should rise slowly as fewer young people become addicted. At some future time, the number of heroin-dependent persons is likely to stabilize at some very low percentage of the population. Several factors should be operative simultaneously to make unlikely any new wave of addiction.

One important but intangible factor is the effect such an action would have on the "mystique" that seems to surround those who use heroin within the population now vulnerable to its appeal. Part of this appeal is through association with the "fast and loose" life-style of the young criminal-addict. With the placement of heroin in pharmacies, the glamor of the big dealer or the addict "living by his wits" will be stripped from the heroin abuser. He will be seen more clearly as someone who has an unfortunate, degrading, and unenviable vice. Given the disproportionate representation of minorities among addicts, it is certain that minority spokesmen will be vocal in their efforts to reinforce that view.

A further indication that, in spite of availability, few people would experiment with heroin comes from a national survey done by the National Commission on Marihuana and Drug Abuse. Fewer than 1 percent of the adults sampled stated that they would "try it" [heroin] if it were "legal and available."[11] Given this finding, it is a reasonable hypothesis that the pool of persons who would experiment with heroin is tiny indeed—regardless of availability—and that from within that small pool, the number of persons who would allow themselves to become addicted is smaller still. While some experimentation may occur, fear and informal pressures should minimize the number of persons who escalate from experimentation to dependency.

Finally, an historical reminder is of interest here. As indicated in chapter 1, the *rate* of addiction to opiates near the turn of this century was approximately the same as now. During this time, not only was there unrestricted access to opiates, but also many heavily promoted remedies containing opiates carried no indication of contents (until the Pure Food and Drug Act of 1906). It is reasonable to assume that many developed their dependency back then through a good-intentioned use of presumably safe medicines. Under the conditions of this alternative, heroin would be sold as such with the warnings noted previously.

What then will be the likely extent or rapidity of decline in heroin addiction under these conditions? Strong informal pressures are likely to bring about a gradual reduction in the number of dependent persons up to a point of relative stability. Most would continue to avoid heroin for the same reason that they do now: its use is strongly disapproved. The draconian sanctions now in existence do not stand as the barrier between abstinence and indulgence; they are merely reflective of a strongly negative consensus of the people about its use. Even in the unlikely event that this consensus were to change, and heroin were to become "respectable," these formal sanctions would be of even less value in their deterrent effect. We are now watching a similar process as attitudes about marijuana have changed considerably in the last few years in spite of the lag in bringing criminal sanctions in line with current expectations.

In conclusion, the possible alternative outlined here seems to offer several advantages over our present approach to the problem of opiate dependence. The paradox, documented by this undertaking, of creating more serious forms of deviance while attempting to suppress opiate use would be eliminated. Although the reintegration of older addicts into a conventional life-style would be (and is) quite difficult, the addicts a generation from now never will have known the life-style of the addict-criminal subculture. In so far as these future addicts may be criminals in the conventional sense, their choice of vice will be quite irrelevant to their criminal careers.

Hopefully, a gradual decline in the number of dependent persons would be an additional tangible benefit. This proposal openly acknowledges the possibility that several hundred thousand persons may be addicted to heroin at any given time. It suggests, however, that such persons are likely to be far more heterogeneous and productive when their only liability is an opiate habit in a culture that no longer labels them as sick or prosecutes them as criminal.

It must be emphasized that the author is aware of the intense opposition that such a proposal would generate. Recognition of that fact, however, should not discourage a scholarly debate of its merits and shortcomings.

Appendixes

Appendix A
Statement of Purpose

Center for the Administration of Justice
College of Public Affairs
The American University
Massachusetts & Nebraska Avenues, N.W.
Washington, D.C. 20016

This interview is part of a study that is attempting to describe the relationship between drug addiction and crime. You will be asked questions about your experiences both before and after you began using drugs. All of these answers will help clarify how narcotic use and crime are related.

You may refuse to answer any question that you find objectionable. We prefer that you refuse to answer a question rather than give a false answer.

You will receive a copy of this form to assure you that all answers will be kept confidential and used for research purposes *only*. The responses of any one person will in no way be traceable.

Philip Baridon
Principal Investigator

Appendix B
Interview Schedule

Question #	Var. #	Col. #	0 = no or no answer
1	001	4	From the time you began regular use of narcotics, how many cities have you lived in? 1 2 3 4 5 6 7 8 > 8
a2	002	5-6	How old were you when you left school? ___ (00-30)
a3	003	7-8	What was the highest grade (year) of regular school you completed excluding a G.E.D.)? ___ (00-17)
4	004	9-14	What is your date of birth? (MMDDYY) ___
___	___	blank	
5	005	16	Were you using heroin or any other narcotic before you left school? yes (1) no (0)
6	006	17	(If the answer to question #5 was yes) Did narcotic use influence your decision to leave school? yes (1) no (0) n/a (5)
7	007	18-19	How old were you when you *first* used heroin or any other narcotic for nonmedical reasons? ___ (08-40)
8	008	20	What drug was that? 1. heroin 2. methadone 3. codeine 4. cough syrup (turp) 5. morphine 6. demerol 7. dilaudid 8. opium 9. other: ___ (0-9)
9	009	21	How were you taking the drug back then? 1. mainlining 2. skinpopping 3. snorting 4. swallowing (0-4)
10	010	22	Who gave you your first shot/dose? 1. A friend by himself 2. A friend with other friends nearby 3. A relative (except spouse) 4. A girlfriend (wife) or boyfriend (husband) 5. A stranger 6. Self-obtained and administered 7. other: specify ___ (0-7)
___	___	blank	
11	011	24-27	Do you know or strongly suspect that the person who gave you that first shot has *ever* been involved with any of these crimes:

Burglary: yes (1) no (0)
Robbery: yes (2) no (0)
Shoplifting/larceny: yes (3) no (0)
Forgery or checks: yes (4) no (0)

(0000-1234) or (9999) for n/a, d/k, rfs

Question #	Var. #	Col. #	
12	012	28-29	How much time passed after the first time you used a narcotic until you knew you had a habit? ___ months (01-99)
13	013	30	Think back to the time when you were just experimenting (chipping) with narcotics (or using for the first time). What were most of your friends doing at that time? 1. Most of your friends were using about *the same* amount of narcotics as you were.

97

Question #	Var. #	Col. #	0 = no or no answer
			2. Most of your friends were using *more* narcotics than you were. 3. *Only a few* of your friends were using narcotics during that time. 4. *None* of your friends were using narcotics. (0-4)
14	014	31	After you became addicted, how much time did you spend with ''straight'' (nonaddict) friends? 1. About the same as before 2. Less than before 3. Much less than before 4. Almost no time 5. Didn't have many friends (0-5)
15	015	32	Try to think back to the time *just before* you began using narcotics. Now think of 5 (or so) friends that you hung around with then. How would you describe the type of activity most of them engaged in? 1. Serious crime (robbery, burglary, etc.) 2. Less serious crime (petty theft, joyriding, gambling, etc.) 3. Very little if any crime 4. n/a (didn't have many friends) (0-4)
16	016	33	How many of these 5 friends eventually became addicted to a narcotic? 0 1 2 3 4 5 9 (no answer) (0-5,9)
17	017	34	After (some of) your friends became addicts, do you think they committed: 1. more crime 2. less crime 3. about the same amount 4. very little crime except dealing (0-4)
—	—	blank	
18	018	36	Do you know any *addicts* who got *most* of their money from: *A.* Robbery? no (0) yes: 1. daily 2. 2-4 times a week 3. about once a week 4. 1-2 times a month 5. d/k how often (0-5)
	019	37	*B.* Burglary? no (0) yes: 1. daily 2. 2-4 times a week. 3. about once a week. 4. 1-2 times a month 5. d/k how often (0-5)
	020	38	*C.* Shoplifting/larceny? no (0) yes: 1. daily 2. almost every day 3. 2-3 times a week 4. about once a week or less 5. d/k how often (0-5)
19	021	39	Do most addicts who support their habit by crime stay with one thing or do they have a lot of hustles? 1. generally one type of offense 2. various offenses 3. offense type depends on habit costs (0-3)
20	022	40	Do you think that burglars and stick-up men who are addicts take more chances (are less careful) than nonaddicts who do the same thing? no (0) yes (1) d/k (2) (0-2)
21	023	41	Do you know any *nonaddicts* who got *most* of their money from. *A.* Robbery? no (0) yes: 1. daily 2. 2-4 times a week 3. about once a week 4. 1-2 times month 5. d/k how often (0-5)
	024	42	*B.* Burglary? no (0) yes: 1/ daily 2. 2-4 times a week 3. about once a week 4. 1-2 times a month 5. d/k how often (0-5)

Question #	Var. #	Col. #	0 = no or no answer
	025	43	C. Shoplifting/larceny? no (0) yes: 1. daily 2. almost every day 3. 2-3 times a week 4. about once a week or less 5. d/k how often (0-5)
22	026	44-45	When you *first* began using narcotics every day, how much was it costing you each day? ___ (01-99)
23	027	46	Respondent indicates drug expenses were: 1. personal cost 2. born by someone else 3. mixed response (0-3)
24	028	47-49	How much did it cost each day one year later? ___ (001-400)
25	029	50-52	How much did it cost each day during the last year you had a habit? ___ (001-400)
	030	53-54	What year was that? ___ (40-74)
26	031	55	Of the addicts that you *knew well*, where did they get *most* of their money? 1. burglary 2. dealing 3. larceny/shoplifting 4. robbery 5. forgery/checks 6. gambling 7. spouse/kin 8. legitimate job 9. other: specify ___ (0-9)
27	032	56	(If an illegitimate source) where they doing (this) before they got hooked on narcotics? no (0) yes (1) mixed response (2) n/a, d/k, or rfs (3) (0-3)
28			Try to remember *before* you began using narcotics. Had you ever done any of these things?
	033	57	A. Truancy from school? no (0) seldom or a few times (1) frequently (2)
	034	58	B. Destroying property? no (0) seldom or a few times (1) frequently (2)
	035	59	C. Car stealing? no (0) seldom or a few times (1) frequently (2)
	036	60	D. Gambling? no (0) seldom or a few times (1) frequently (2)
	037	61	E. Shoplifting/larceny no (0) seldom or a few times (1) frequently (2)
	038	62	F. Fighting with weapons? no (0) seldom or a few times (1) frequently (2)
	039	63	G. Burglary/housebreaking? no (0) seldom or a few times (1) frequently (2)
	040	64	H. Robbery (armed or unarmed)? no (0) seldom or a few times (1) frequently (2)
———	———	blank	
29			When your habit began to get expensive, what were your sources of money? (Indicate frequency)
	041	66	A. Burglary ___ 0 = never
	042	67	B. Dealing ___ 1 = seldom (irregular work)
	043	68	C. Larceny/ shoplifting ___ 2 = frequently (regular P.T. job)

Question #	Var. #	Col. #	0 = no or no answer
	044	69	D. Forgery/checks ____ 3 = very frequently
	045	70	E. Robbery ____ (F.T. job)
	046	71	F. Gambling ____ 5 = rfs
	047	72	G. Spouse/kin/friends ____
	048	73	H. Legitimate job ____ Type work ____
	049	74	I. Other: specify ____
—	—	blank (75-78)	
n/a	n/a	79-80	card number 01
30	050	7-8	How many times have you personally been arrested for *anything* except disorderly or traffic charges? ____ (00-99)
31			Do you remember what the police charged you with and about what year it was?

			Charge	# of times arrested	year of first arrest
	051-052	9-11	A. Burglary	(0-9) ____	(40-74) ____
	053-054	12-14	B. Robbery	(0-9) ____	(40-74) ____
	055-056	15-17	C. Larceny	(0-9) ____	(40-74) ____
	057-058	18-20	D. Drug related incl. PIE & PIC	(0-9) ____	(40-74) ____
	059-060	21-23	E. Rec. stolen prop.	(0-9) ____	(40-74) ____
	061-062	25-27	F. Forgery/checks	(0-9) ____	(40-74) ____
	063-064	28-30	G. Aggravated assault or murder	(0-9) ____	(40-74) ____
	065-066	31-33	H. Auto theft	(0-9) ____	(40-74) ____
	067-068	34-36	I. Prostitution or procuring	(0-9) ____	(40-74) ____
	069-070	37-39	J. Other: ____	(0-9) ____	(40-74) ____
——	——	blank			

32	071	41	When drug costs go up fast either because of tolerance or higher prices, do you think most addicts: 1. Control their habit? Use less stuff? 2. Take a cure? (Treatment, jail, or successful cold turkey) 3. Hustle for more money? 4. Begin mixing (opiates) with cheaper drugs? (0-4)
33	072	42	Did you ever begin to feel that your habit was getting out of hand (too expensive)? no (0) yes (1) rfs (9) (0-1,9)
	073	43-44	(If yes) What year was that ____ (40-74)
34	074	45	(For yes answer) What did you do about it? 1. Control your habit? Use less stuff? 2. Take a cure? 3. Hustle for more money? 4. Begin mixing (opiates) with cheaper drugs? (0-4)

Question #	Var. #	Col. #	0 = no or no answer
35	075	46-47	How many total years have you been addicted to street drugs (not including time in institutions (jails) or in drug treatment programs)? ____ years (01-99)
36	076	48-49	How old were you the last time you had a habit from street narcotics? ____ (15-60)
37	077	50	When do you think most addicts commit their crimes? 1. When they are high? 2. When they are "coming down" or just "getting over"? 3. When they are starting to get sick? 4. Varies-no pattern (0-4)
38	078	51	(If appropriate) How did you usually feel during a hustle? 1. Was high 2. Was "coming down" or just "getting over" 3. Was getting sick 4. Varied-no pattern (0-4)
39	079	52	Do you think that using heroin makes addicts more or less likely to get busted than a nonaddict committing the same crime? 1. more likely 2. less likely 3. no difference (0-3)
——	——	blank	
40	080	54	Did you come to NTA as a: 1. volunteer? 2. through court referral? 3. other: ____ (0-3)
41	081	55	Are you now on: 1. methadone maintenance? 2. detox? 3. other: ____ (0-3)
42	082	56-57	Are there any questions that you minded? (If yes, which?) ____ (00-40)
a43	083	58-59	If we interviewed your friends, do you think there are any questions where they would not tell the truth?·(If yes, which?) ____ (00-40)
44	084	60	Sex of respondent: 1. male 2. female
45	085	61	Race of respondent: 1. black 2. white 3. other
——	——	blank	(62-78)
n/a	n/a	79-80	card number 02

---

a Indicates that the question was taken either unchanged or essentially unchanged from the Johns Hopkins survey as a check on sample representativeness.

Appendix C
Comparison of Official Arrest Records with Self-reported Listing of Arrests

Addict Sequence #	Self-report	D.C. Records
005	Narcotics possession (1)—1970	Narcotics possession (1)—1971
	Gambling (2)—1963	——
012	Narcotics possession (1)—1973	——
019	Narcotics possession (2)—1969	Narcotics possession (1)—1969
	Forgery (false pretense) (1)—1969	False pretense (forgery) (1)—1969
	Robbery (1)—1969	——
	——	Petit larceny (1)—1970
	Auto theft (1)—1964	——
027	Narcotics possession (2)—1970	——
	Receiving stolen property (1)—1973	——
034	Larceny (16)—1955	Larceny (14)—1956
	Burglary (1)—1965	Burglary (1)—1964
	——	Attempt burglary (1)—1968
	——	Narcotics possession (1)—1961
	——	Simple assault (1)—1955
042	Forgery (1)—1973	——
047	Larceny (1)—1973	——
054	Assault (1)—1972	——
061	——	——
068	Narcotics possession (3)—1968	Narcotics possession (1)—1970
	Burglary (2)—1968	——
	Larceny (1)—1973	——
	Assault (1)—1973	——
075	Larceny (1)—1972	Larceny (1)—1972
	——	Destroying property (1)—1965

Addict Sequence #	Self-report	D.C. Records
082	Robbery (1)—1974	——
091	Robbery (1)—1936	——
	Narcotics vagrancy (1)—1958	Narcotics vagrancy (2)—1957
098	Forgery (1)—1973	——

Note: Numbers in parentheses refer to total arrests for that offense. Years indicate only the first arrest for that offense.

Notes

Notes

Chapter 1
An Overview of Opiate Addiction and Crime

1. T.D. Crothers, "Medicolegal Relations of Opium Inebriety and the Necessity for Legal Recognition," *Journal of the American Medical Association (J.A.M.A.)*, 18 August 1900.

2. Frederick Baldi, "The Drug Habit and the Underworld," *J.A.M.A.*, 23 December 1916.

3. Webb v. U.S., 249 U.S. 96 (1919).
Jin Fuey Moy v. U.S., 254 U.S. 189 (1920).
U.S. v. Behrman, 258 U.S. 280 (1922).

4. H. Brill, "History of the Medical Treatment of Drug Dependence" (Unpublished paper prepared for the National Commission on Marihuana and Drug Abuse, 1973).

5. *Indiana Penal Code*, Ch. 35, sec. 10-3538a.

6. Robinson v. California, 370 U.S. 660 (1962).

7. David Musto, *The American Disease* (New Haven: Yale University Press, 1973).

8. "The Struggle of Mankind against its Deadliest Foe," broadcast by NBC March 1928, printed in *Narcotic Education* 1:51-54 (1928).

9. Mary Bailey, "Drug Peddling, Addiction, and Criminalism," *Journal of Criminal Law and Criminology* 23 (1932).

10. Twain Michelsen, "Lindesmith's Mythology," *Journal of Criminal Law and Criminology* 31 (1940).

11. P. Cushman, "Methadone Maintenance in Hard-Core Criminal Addicts: Economic Effects," *New York State Journal of Medicine* 71 (July 15, 1971).

12. R.L. Dupont, "Heroin Addiction Treatment and Crime Reduction," *American Journal of Psychiatry* 128, no. 7 (1972).

13. Erich Goode, *Drugs in American Society* (New York: Knopf, 1972).

14. Edmund Muskie, "Crime, Drugs, and the Nation," *Journal of Drug Issues* 2, no. 2 (Spring 1972).

15. K.P. O'Brien and R.C. Sullivan, "The Addict Today—1970," *Police* 14, no. 5 (1970).

16. Benjamin Malcolm, "Detoxification of 20,000 Addicts," *Proceedings of the National Association for the Prevention of Addiction to Narcotics* (San Francisco: January 1972).

17. Philip Baridon, "A Comparative Analysis of Drug Addiction in 33 Countries," *Drug Forum* 2, no. 4 (1973).

18. BNDD, *Director's Report* (Washington: U.S. Department of Justice, Bureau of Narcotics and Dangerous Drugs, March 31, 1973).

19. Joseph Seifter, "Pharmacology of Heroin," in *Proposal for the Use of Diacetyl Morphine (Heroin) in the Treatment of Heroin Dependent Individuals* (New York: Unpublished proposal by the Vera Foundation, May 1972).

20. Ibid.

21. Ibid.
   James DeLong, "The Drugs and Their Effects," in *Dealing With Drug Abuse*, A Report to the Ford Foundation (New York: Praeger, 1972).

22. Ibid.

23. Raymond Shafer, *Drug Use in America: Problem in Perspective*, Second Report of the National Commission on Marihuana and Drug Abuse (Washington: U.S. Government Printing Office, 1973).

24. Ibid.

25. Alfred Lindesmith, *Addiction and Opiates* (Chicago: Aldine Publishing, 1968).

26. Nolan, "The Opium Habit," *Catholic World* 33 (1881).

27. J.A. O'Hara, "Use and Abuse of Drugs in Treatment of Addicts," *New Orleans Medicine and Surgery Journal* 72 (1919).

28. Robert Norris, "Historical-Legal Background of Drug Use," *California Probation, Parole, and Correctional Association Journal* 5, no. 2 (1968).

29. C.E. Sandoz, "Report on Morphinism to the Municipal Court of Boston," *Journal of Criminal Law and Criminology* 13 (1922).

30. Lawrence Kolb, "Drug Addiction in its Relation to Crime," *Mental Hygiene* 9, no. 1 (1925).

31. P. Anchersen, "On the Prognosis of Narcomania," *Acta Psychiatrica et Neurologica* 22, no. 3/4 (1947).

32. R.N. Chopra and G.S. Chopra, "Opium Habit in India: Studies on the Physical and Mental Effects Produced by Opium Addiction," *Indian Journal of Medical Research* 23, no. 2 (October 1935).

33. R.N. Chopra and I.C. Chopra, "Quasi-Medical Use of Opium in India and its Effects," *U.N. Bulletin on Narcotics* 7 (1955).

34. Comprehensive Drug Abuse Prevention and Control Act of 1970, Public Law 91-513, 91st Congress.

35. Edgar May, "Narcotics Addiction and Control in Great Britain," in *Dealing with Drug Abuse*, A Report to the Ford Foundation (New York: Praeger, 1972).

36. Nicholas Kittrie, *The Right To Be Different* (Baltimore: Johns Hopkins Press, 1971).

37. May, "Narcotics Addition."

38. J.E. Glancy, "The Treatment of Narcotic Dependence in the United Kingdom," *Bulletin on Narcotics* 24, no. 4 (1972).

39. Gila Hayim et al., *Heroin Use and Crime in a Methadone Maintenance Program*, An Interim Report, U.S. Department of Justice, Law Enforcement Assistance Administration (Washington: U.S. Government Printing Office, 1973).

40. John Lister, "Drugs of Addiction—The Ciba Foundation—A Century of Antisepsis," *New England Journal of Medicine* 272, no. 21 (1967).

41. Pierce James, "Delinquency and Heroin Addiction in Britain," *British Journal of Criminology* 9, no. 2 (1969).

42. James Zacune et al. "Heroin Use in a Provincial Town—One Year Later," *International Journal of the Addictions* 4, no. 2 (1969).

43. John Ball and William Bates, "Migration and Residential Mobility of Narcotic Drug Addicts," *Social Problems* 14, no. 1 (1966).

44. S. Yurok, "The Economics of the Skag Trade," *D.C. Gazette* 2, no. 13 (April 26, 1971).

45. Herbert Berger, "Conference on Narcotic Addiction,

Patiela House, New Delhi, Republic of India," *International Journal of the Addictions* 2, no. 2 . (1967).

46. Charles Winick, "Physician Narcotic Addicts," *Social Problems* 9, no. 2 (Fall 1961).

47. Shafer, *Drug Use*.

48. David Matza, *Delinquency and Drift* (New York: Wiley, 1964).

49. Hayim. *Heroin Use*.

50. May, "Narcotics Addiction."

51. Winick, "Physician Narcotic Addicts."

52. David Maurer and Victor Vogel, *Narcotics and Narcotic Addiction*, 3rd ed. (Springfield: C.C. Thomas, 1970).

53. Shafer, *Drug Use*.

54. Takemitsu Hemmi, "Narcotic-Addict Prisoners in Japan," *Corrective Psychiatry and Journal of Social Therapy* 11, no. 2 (1965).

55. J.P. Morgan, "Drug Addiction: Criminal or Medical Problem?" *Police* 9, no. 6 (1965).

56. *Narcotics and Drug Abuse*, Task Force Report (Washington: U.S. Government Printing Office, 1967).

57. Maurer and Vogel, *Narcotics*.

58. G.E. Vaillant and L. Brill, "A Twelve-Year Follow-Up of New York City Addicts: The Relation of Treatment to Outcome" (Paper presented at the Annual Meeting of the American Psychiatric Association, New York City, May 3, 1965).

59. John O'Donnell, "Narcotic Addiction and Crime," *Social Problems* 13, no. 4 (1966).

60. Hayim, *Heroin Use*.

61. O'Donnell, "Narcotic Addiction and Crime."

62. Roger Hood and Richard Sparks, *Key Issues in Criminology* (New York: McGraw-Hill, 1970).

63. Hayim, *Heroin Use*.

64. J.A. Inciardi, and C.D. Chambers, "Self Reported Criminal Behavior of Narcotic Addicts" (Paper presented at the 33rd Annual Meeting of the Committee on Problems of Drug Dependence, Toronto, Canada, 1971).

65. "Special Mental Health Problems of Urban Life: Drug Abuse," in *The Mental Health of Urban America*, U.S. National Institute of Mental Health Public Health Service. Publication #1906 (Washington: U.S. Government Printing Office, 1969).

66. Hayim, *Heroin Use*.

67. Ibid.

68. Goode, *Drugs*.

69. I.H. Page, "Further Evidence on Methadone and Criminal Drug Addicts," *Modern Medicine* 37, no. 5 (1969).

70. Vincent P. Dole, Marie E. Nyswanden, and Alan Warner, "Successful Treatment of 750 Criminal Addicts," *Journal of the American Medical Association* 206, no. 12 (1968).

71. Richard Phillipson, "Methadone Maintenance: Why Continue Controls?" in *Proceedings*, Third National Conference on Methadone Treatment (Rockville, Md.: National Institute of Mental Health, November 1970).

72. Herman Joseph, "A Probation Department Treats Heroin Addicts," *Federal Probation* 37, no. 1 (March 1973).

73. Hayim, *Heroin Use*.

74. Ibid.

75. C.E. Beech and A.I. Gregersen, "Three-Year Follow-Up Study—Drug Addiction Clinic, Mimico," *Canadian Journal of Corrections* 6, no. 2 (April 1964).

76. Hayim, *Heroin Use*.

77. Marshall Clinard, *Sociology of Deviant Behavior*, 3rd ed. (New York: Holt, Rinehart, and Winston, 1968).

Chapter 3
Research Findings: Descriptive

1. Kenneth L. Jones, Louis W. Shainberg, and Curtis O. Byer, *Drugs and Alcohol* (New York: Harper and Row, 1969).

2. Seifter, "Pharmacology of Heroin."

Chapter 4
Research Findings: Analysis and Discussion

1. Statistics and Evaluation Division, Department of Human Resources, Washington, D.C.

2. Urbane F. Bass, Velma W. Brock, Barry S. Brown, and Robert L. Dupont, "A Study of Narcotics Addicted Offenders at the D.C. Jail" (Washington: Unpublished study by the Narcotics Treatment Administration, 1973).

3. Gila Hayim, *Changes in the Criminal Behavior of Heroin Addicts: A Two-Year Follow-Up of Methadone Treatment* (The Harvard Center for Criminal Justice, 1973).

Chapter 5
Summary and Conclusions

1. M. Hindelang et al., *Source Book of Criminal Justice Statistics 1973*, table 4.3 (Washington: U.S. Government Printing Office, 1973).

2. Shafer, *Drug Use*.

3. Ibid.

4. Milan Karcok, "War on Heroin—Proclamations of Victory Premature," *The Journal* 3, no. 11 (1974).

5. Ibid.

6. Leslie T. Wilkins, "A General Theory of Deviance," in *Social Deviance* (Englewood Cliffs: Prentice-Hall, 1965).

7. Alan Massam, "Doubt and Uncertainty Cloud Apparent Success of 'British System,'" *The Journal* 3, no. 12 (1974).

8. J. Mott and M. Taylor, *Delinquency Amongst Opiate Users* (London: Her Majesty's Stationery Office, 1974).

9. Ibid.

10. C.E. Riordan and L.C. Gould, *A Proposal for the Use of Diacetyl Morphine (Heroin) in the Treatment of Heroin-Dependent Individuals* (Unpublished proposal by the Vera Foundation, May 1972).

11. Shafer, *Drug Use*.

Bibliography

Bibliography

Alksne, Lieberman, and Brill. 1967. "A Conceptual Model of the Life Cycle of Addiction." *International Journal of the Addictions* 2, no 2.

An Evaluation of Treatment Programs for Drug Abusers. 1973. Interdrug/Final Report, vol. 2. The Johns Hopkins University School of Hygiene and Public Health.

Anchersen, P. 1947. "On the Prognosis of Narcomania." *Acta Psychiatrica et Neurologica* 22, no. 3/4.

Bacon, Frank. 1960. "Prevention of Crime Due to Heroin Dependence." *Medical Annals of the District of Columbia* 38, no. 4.

Bailey, Mary. 1932. "Drug Peddling, Addiction, and Criminalism." *Journal of Criminal Law and Criminology* 23.

Baldi, Frederick. December 23, 1916. "The Drug Habit and the Underworld." *Journal of the American Medical Association (J.A.M.A.).*

Ball, John. 1971. "The Reliability and Validity of Interview Data Obtained from 59 Narcotic Drug Addicts." *American Journal of Sociology* 72, no. 6.

Ball, John, and Bates, William. 1966. "Migration and Residential Mobility of Narcotic Drug Addicts." *Social Problems* 14, no. 1.

Baridon, Philip. 1973. "A Comparative Analysis of Drug Addiction in 33 Countries." *Drug Forum* 2, no. 4.

Bass, Urbane F., Brock, Velma W., Brown, Barry S. and Dupont, Robert L. 1973. "A Study of Narcotics Addicted Offenders at the D.C. Jail" (Unpublished study by the Narcotics Treatment Administration).

Battegay, R. 1961. "Comparative Investigations of the Genesis of Alcoholism and Drug Addiction." *U.N. Bulletin on Narcotics* 13, no. 2.

Beech, C.E., and Gregersen, A.I. April 1964. "Three-Year Follow-Up Study—Drug Addiction Clinic, Mimico." *Canadian Journal of Corrections* 6, no. 2.

Berger, Herbert. 1967. "Conference on Narcotic Addiction, Patiela House, New Delhi, Republic of India." *International Journal of the Addictions* 2, no. 2.

115

Bishop, Ernest. July 1919. "Narcotic Drug Addiction: A Public Health Problem." *American Journal of Public Health* 9, no. 7.

Blumberg, Herbert W., Cohen, S. Daryl, Dronfield, B. Elizabeth, Mordecai, Elizabeth A., Roberts, J. Colin and Hawks, David. In press. "British Opiate Users: People Approaching London Drug Treatment Centers." *International Journal of the Addictions.*

Brill, H. 1973. "History of the Medical Treatment of Drug Dependence" (Unpublished paper prepared for the National Commission on Marihuana and Drug Abuse).

Brown, B., and Brewster, G. In press. "A Comparison of Addict Clients Retained and Lost to Treatment." *International Journal of the Addictions.*

Brown, Barry, Gauvey, Susan, Meyers, Marilyn and Stark, Steven. 1971. "In Their Own Words: Addicts' Reasons for Initiating and Withdrawing from Heroin." *International Journal of the Addictions* 6, no. 4.

Bureau of Narcotics and Dangerous Drugs (BNDD). March 31, 1973. *Director's Report.* Washington: U.S. Department of Justice.

Chase, Lillian. "Ontario." 1961. *Canadian Medical Association Journal* (Toronto) 84, no. 14.

Chein, Isidor, Gerard, Donald L., Lee, Robert S. and Rosenfeld, Eva. 1964. *The Road of H: Narcotics, Delinquency, and Social Policy.* New York: Basic Books.

Cherubin, C.E. et al. Spring 1968. "The Epidermiology of 'Skin Popping' in New York City." *International Journal of the Addictions* 3.

Chopra, R.N., and Chopra, G.S. October 1935. "Opium Habit in India: Studies of the Physical and Mental Effects Produced by Opium Addiction." *Indian Journal of Medical Research* 23, no. 2.

Chopra, R.N., and Chopra, I.C. 1955. "Quasi-Medical Use of Opium and Its Effects." *U.N. Bulletin on Narcotics* 7.

Clinard, Marshall. 1968. *Sociology of Deviant Behavior* 3rd ed. New York: Holt, Rinehart, and Winston.

Craig, S., and Brown, B. 1973. "Comparison of Youthful Heroin Users and Non-Users from the Same Community" (Unpublished manuscript).

Crothers, T.D. August 18, 1900. "Medicolegal Relations of Opium

Inebriety and the Necessity for Legal Recognition." *Journal of the American Medical Association*.

Cushman, P. July 15, 1971. "Methadone Maintenance in Hard-Core Criminal Addicts: Economic Effects." *New York State Journal of Medicine* 71.

Davis, W.M., and Khalsa, J.H. 1971. "Some Determinants of Aggressive Behavior Induced by Morphine Withdrawal." *Psychonomic Science* 23, no. 1.

DeLong, James. 1972. "The Drugs and Their Effects." In *Dealing With Drug Abuse*, a Report to the Ford Foundation. New York: Praeger.

Dole, Vincent P., Nyswander, Marie E., and Warner, Alan. 1968. "Successful Treatment of 750 Criminal Addicts." *Journal of the American Medical Association* 206, no. 12.

Drug Addiction Among Young Persons in Chicago. 1953. Illinois Institute for Juvenile Research: Chicago Area Project.

Dupont, R.L. 1972. "Heroin Addiction Treatment and Crime Reduction." *American Journal of Psychiatry* 128, no. 7.

Finestone, Harold. 1957. "Narcotics and Criminality." *Law and Contemporary Problems* 22, no. 1.

Fort, Joel. 1969. *The Pleasure Seekers: The Drug Crisis, Youth, and Society*. Indianapolis: Bobbs-Merrill.

Glancy, J.E. 1972. "The Treatment of Narcotic Dependence in the United Kingdom." *Bulletin on Narcotics* 24, no. 4.

Goode, Erich. 1972. *Drugs in American Society*. New York: Knopf.

Gordon, Alistair. 1973. "Patterns of Delinquency in Drug Addiction." *British Journal of Psychiatry* 122.

Hayim, Gila. July 1973. *Changes in the Criminal Behavior of Heroin Addicts: A Two-Year Follow-Up of Methadone Treatment*, Final Report (Unpublished study by The Harvard Law School for Criminal Justice and the Columbia University Addiction Research and Treatment Team).

Hayim, Gila et al. 1973. *Heroin Use and Crime in a Methadone Maintenance Program*, An Interim Report, U.S. Department of Justice, Law Enforcement Assistance Administration. Washington: U.S. Government Printing Office.

Helpern, M., and Rho, Y. 1966. "Deaths from Narcoticism in New York City: Incidence, Circumstances, and Post-Mortem Findings." *New York State Journal of Medicine* 66, no. 18.

Hemmi, Takemitsu. 1965. "Narcotic-Addict Prisoners in Japan." *Corrective Psychiatry and Journal of Social Therapy* 11, no. 2.

Hentoff, N. 1968. *A Doctor Among the Addicts*. Chicago: Rand McNally.

Hindelang, M. et al. 1973. *Source Book of Criminal Justice Statistics*. Washington: U.S. Government Printing Office.

Hood, Roger, and Sparks, Richard. 1970. *Key Issues in Criminology*. New York: McGraw-Hill.

Inciardi, J.A., and Chambers, C.D. 1971. "Self-Reported Criminal Behavior of Narcotic Addicts" (Paper presented at the 33rd Annual Meeting of the Committee on Problems of Drug Dependence, Toronto, Canada).

————. 1972. "Unreported Criminal Involvement of Narcotic Addicts." *Journal of Drug Issues* 2, no. 2.

"Is Methadone Money Well Spent?" 1969. *Medical World News* 10, no. 33.

James, Pierce. 1969. "Delinquency and Heroin Addiction in Britain." *British Journal of Criminology* 9, no. 2.

Jones, Kenneth L., Shainberg, Louis W., and Byer, Curtis D. 1969. *Drugs and Alcohol*. New York: Harper and Row.

Joseph, Herman. March 1973. "A Probation Department Treats Heroin Addicts." *Federal Probation* 37, no. 1.

Kane, John. 1966. *Drug Addiction*. Chicago: Claretian Publications.

Karcok, Milan. 1974. "War on Heroin—Proclamations of Victory Premature." *The Journal* 3, no. 11.

Kolb, Lawrence. 1925. "Drug Addiction in its Relation to Crime." *Mental Hygiene* 9, no. 1.

Kozel, Nicholas, Dupont, Robert L., and Brown, Barry S. 1972. "Narcotics and Crime: A Study of Narcotic Involvement in an Offender Population." *International Journal of the Addictions* 7, no. 3.

Kramer, John. Fall 1971. "Introduction to the Problem of Heroin Addiction in America." *Journal of Psychedelic Drugs* 4, no. 1.

Lindesmith, Alfred. 1965. *The Addict and the Law*. Indiana University Press: Vintage Book.

————. 1968. *Addiction and Opiates*. Chicago: Aldine Publishing Company.

Lister, John. 1967. "Drugs of Addiction—The Ciba Foundation—A Century of Antisepsis." *New England Journal of Medicine* 272, no. 21.

Maddux, James. 1967. "Treatment of Narcotic Addiction." In *Vocational Rehabilitation Administration: Rehabilitating the Narcotic Addict.* Washington: U.S. Government Printing Office.

Malcolm, Benjamin. January 1972. "Detoxification of 20,000 Addicts." *Proceedings of the National Association for the Prevention of Addiction to Narcotics*, San Francisco.

Massam, Alan. 1974. "Doubt and Uncertainty Cloud Apparent Success of the 'British System.'" *The Journal* 3, no. 12.

Matza, David. 1966. *Delinquency and Drift.* New York: Wiley.

Maurer, David, and Vogel, Victor. 1970. *Narcotics and Narcotic Addiction.* 3rd ed. Springfield: C.C. Thomas.

May, Edgar. 1972. "Narcotics Addiction and Control in Great Britain." In *Dealing With Drug Abuse*, A Report to the Ford Foundation. New York: Praeger.

McNamara, Joseph D. 1973. "The History of United States Anti-Opium Policy." *Federal Probation* 37, no. 2.

Messinger, E., and Zitrin, A. 1965. "A Statistical Study of Criminal Drug Addicts." *Crime and Delinquency* 11, no. 3.

Michelsen, Twain. 1940. "Lindesmith's Mythology." *Journal of Criminal Law and Criminology* 31.

Morgan, J.P. 1965. "Drug Addiction: Criminal or Medical Problem?" *Police* 9, no. 6.

Mott, J., and Taylor, M. 1974. *Delinquency Amongst Opiate Users.* London: Her Majesty's Stationery Office.

Muskie, Edmund. Spring 1972. "Crime, Drugs, and the Nation." *Journal of Drug Issues* 2, no. 2.

Musto, David. 1973. *The American Disease.* New Haven: Yale University Press.

"Narcotic Drug Addiction." 1915. *American Medicine* 21, no. 12.

Narcotics and Drug Abuse. 1967. Task Force Report. Washington: U.S. Government Printing Office.

Nolan. 1881. "The Opium Habit." *Catholic World* 33.

Norman, D.J. 1967. *Drug Addiction Research Programme.* Hong Kong: Government Press.

Norris, Robert. 1968. "Historical-Legal Background of Drug Use." *California Probation, Parole and Correctional Association Journal* 5, no. 2.

O'Brien, K.P., and Sullivan, R.C. 1970. "The Addict Today— 1970." *Police* 14, no. 5.

O'Donnell, John. 1966. "Narcotic Addiction and Crime." *Social Problems* 13, no. 4.

_____. 1969. "Patterns of Drug Abuse and their Social Consequences." In *Drugs and Youth* by J. Wittenborn. Springfield: C.C. Thomas.

O'Hara, J.A. 1919. "Use and Abuse of Drugs in Treatment of Addicts." *New Orleans Medicine and Surgery Journal* 72.

Page, I.H. 1969. "Further Evidence on Methadone and Criminal Drug Addicts." *Modern Medicine* 37, no. 5.

Pet, Donald. 1968. "Socio-Cultural Implications of Drug Abuse." In *Drug Abuse: A Course for Educators* by M. Weinswig. Indianapolis: Butler University Press.

Phillipson, Richard. November 1970. "Methadone Maintenance: Why Continue Controls?" In *Proceedings of the Third National Conference on Methadone Treatment*, National Institute of Mental Health, Rockville, Maryland.

Plair, W., and Jackson, L. 1970. *Narcotic Use and Crime: A Report on Interviews with 50 Addicts Under Treatment*. Research Report No. 33. D.C. Department of Corrections.

Preble, E., and Casey, J. March 1969. "Taking Care of Business-the Heroin User's Life on the Street." *International Journal of the Addictions* 4, no. 1.

"The Problem of Dope." January 16, 1956. *Time* 67.

Richman, Alex. April 1966. "Follow-Up of Criminal Narcotic Addicts." *Canadian Psychiatric Association Journal* 11.

Richman, A., Borschneck, A. and Rienzi, A. 1964. "Natural History of Narcotic Addiction." *Canadian Psychiatric Association* (Ottawa) 9, no. 5.

Robins, L.N., and Murphy, G.E. 1967. "Drug Use in a Normal Population of Young Negro Men." *American Journal of Public Health* 57, no. 9.

Rubington, E. 1967. "Drug Addiction as a Deviant Career." *International Journal of the Addictions* 2, no. 1.

Sandoz, C.E. 1922. "Report on Morphinism to the Municipal Court of Boston." *Journal of Criminal Law and Criminology* 13.

Schur, Edwin. 1965. *Crimes Without Victims*. Englewood Cliffs: Prentice-Hall.

Seifter, Joseph. May 1972. "Pharmacology of Heroin." In *Proposal for the Use of Diacetyl Morphine (Heroin) in the Treatment of Heroin Dependent Individuals* (Unpublished proposal by the Vera Foundation, New York).

Shafer, Raymond. 1973. *Drug Use in America: Problem in Perspective*, Second Report of the National Commission on Marihuana and Drug Abuse. Washington: U.S. Government Printing Office.

"Sociological Study of Male Patients and Dischargees." 1969. In *Society for the Aid and Rehabilitation of Drug Addicts, Annual Report*. Hong Kong.

Spear, H.B., and Glatt, M.M. 1971. "The Influence of Canadian Addicts on Heroin Addiction in the United Kingdom." *British Journal of Addiction* 6, no. 2.

"Special Mental Health Problems of Urban Life: Drug Abuse." 1969. In *The Mental Health of Urban America*. U.S. National Institute of Mental Health Public Health Service Publication #1906. Washington: U.S. Government Printing Office.

Stephens, R., and Levine, S. 1973. "Crime and Narcotic Addiction." In *Applied Psychology in Law Enforcement and Corrections*. Springfield: C.C. Thomas.

U.S., Congress, House, Subcommittee No. 4 of the Committee on the Judiciary. 1972.

"The Struggle of Mankind against Its Deadliest Foe," 1928. Broadcast by NBC, 1 March, 1928, printed in *Narcotic Education* 1.

Treatment and Rehabilitation of Narcotic Addicts: Hearings. 92nd Cong. 2nd sess. Serial no. 14, p. 2. Washington: U.S. Government Printing Office.

U.S., Congress, Senate, Committee on Government Operations. 1971. *Drug Abuse Prevention and Control: Joint Hearings*. 92nd Cong., 1st sess. Washington: U.S. Government Printing Office.

Vaillant, G.E., and Brill, L. May 3, 1965. "A Twelve-Year Follow-Up of New York City Addicts: The Relation of Treatment to Outcome" (Paper presented at the Annual Meeting of the American Psychiatric Association, New York City).

Weissman, James C., Katsampes, Paul L., and Giacinti, Thomas A. March 1974. "Opiate Use and Criminality Among A Jail Population" (Unpublished paper presented at the National Drug Abuse Conference).

Wilkins, Leslie T. 1965. "A General Theory of Deviance." In *Social Deviance*. Englewood Cliffs: Prentice-Hall.

Wilson, Moore, and Wheat. Fall 1972. "The Problem of Heroin." *The Public Interest* 29,

Winick, Charles. Fall 1961. "Physician Narcotic Addicts." *Social Problems* 9, no 2.

―――. Spring 1962, "The Lifecycle of the Narcotic Addict and of Addiction." *U.N. Bulletin on Narcotics* 14, no. 5.

―――. 1970. "Drug Addiction and Crime." In *Readings on Drug Use and Abuse* by B.Q. Hafen. Provo, Utah: Brigham Young University Press.

Yurok, S. April 26, 1971. "The Economics of the Skag Trade." *D.C. Gazette* 2, no. 13.

Zacune, James, et. al. 1969. "Heroin Use in a Provincial Town― One Year Later." *International Journal of the Addictions* 4.

Zimmering, P., and Toolan, J. 1952. "Drug Addiction in Adolescents." *Journal of Nervous and Mental Diseases* 116, no. 3.

Index

Index

addict population size, 3, 11, 57
addict profiles: general, 29-32, 37-49, 79-80, 82-83; individual, 32-38
addiction as a cause of crime, 1-3, 5-7. *See also* property crime and addiction
addict versus nonaddict crime, xviii-xix, 40-41, 58-59, 68, 75-77
age, addiction, and crime, xviii, 12, 18, 23, 25-26, 63-65, 69-71, 82
alternatives and policy recommendations, 85-91

Brill, L.J., 17
Bureau of Narcotics and Dangerous Drugs, 10-11, 51, 54-55, 60. *See also* Drug Enforcement Administration

crime rate fluctuations, 54-57
criminal addict—confirmed, xx, 15-16, 23-25, 32, 63, 67-70, 72-73, 81-82. *See also* addict typologies
criminal addict—marginal, xx, 15, 24, 32, 63, 67-70, 72-73, 81. *See also* addict typologies

dealing, 44-45, 66, 75
deviance amplification, xviii, 86-88. *See also* social policy and addict crime
Dole, Vincent P., 22
Drug Abuse Council, 85
Drug Enforcement Administration, 51

Goode, Erich, 21
Great Britain and addiction control, 6-10, 86-87

Hayim, Gila, 21, 23-24, 84

Heroin: addiction time, 39; cost of, 10-11, 42-43, 52-54, 58-62, 65-66; pharmacological effects, 4-5, 39; quality/potency/purity, 39, 57-60, 81

law enforcement efforts to control addict crime, 2-4, 11, 54-60, 81, 83, 85-86
legitimate junkie, 14. *See also* addict typologies

Maurer, David, 16, 18
medical addict, 14-15. *See also* addict typologies
methadone maintenance, 2-23, 57-59, 81
methodology, xix-xxii, 27-32, 39-77

naive addict, 14-16, 32, 67-68, 72. *See also* addict typologies
Narcotics Treatment Administration, xx-xxi, 27-28, 30-31, 33-34, 57-58, 60-65
National Commission on Marihuana and Drug Abuse, 2, 16-17, 85, 89. *See also* Shafer Commission
non-causal relationship between addiction and crime, 6, 16-20. *See also* preaddictive criminality
Nyswander, Marie E., 22

O'Donnell, John A., 18-19
old man, 16. *See also* addict typologies
opiate price and gainful/property crime, xvii-xix, 42, 47, 49, 51-54, 56-57, 59-63, 80

postaddictive criminality, 19-22, 43-47, 63, 67-76, 82-85
preaddictive criminality, xviii, 16-20, 22, 24, 40, 43-45, 67-76, 82

About the Author

Philip C. Baridon received the M.A. and Ph.D. in criminal justice from the School of Criminal Justice at The State University of New York at Albany. He is presently a senior consultant in Planning Research Corporation, Public Management Services, Inc., Mc-Lean, Virginia. Prior to that, he taught for approximately two years at The American University, The Center for the Administration of Justice. Dr. Baridon also served as a patrolman in Washington, D.C. for four years. His publications include "A Comparative Analysis of Drug Addiction in 33 Countries," *Drug Forum* 2, no. 4 (1973).

Related Lexington Books

Hannan, Timothy H., *The Economics of Methadone Maintenance*, 192 pp., 1975

Light, Patricia K., *Let the Children Speak*, 128 pp., 1975

Moore, Mark H., *Buy and Bust*, In Press

Rachin, Richard L., Czajkoski, Eugene, *Drug Abuse Control*, 208 pp., 1975

Teff, Harvey, *Drugs, Society, and the Law*, 224 pp., 1975

Zusman, Jack, Wurster, Cecil, *Program Evaluation*, 304 pp., 1975.